BASIC
COUNSELLING
SKILLS

SAGE | 50 YEARS

SAGE was founded in 1965 by Sara Miller McCune to support the dissemination of usable knowledge by publishing innovative and high-quality research and teaching content. Today, we publish more than 850 journals, including those of more than 300 learned societies, more than 800 new books per year, and a growing range of library products including archives, data, case studies, reports, and video. SAGE remains majority-owned by our founder, and after Sara's lifetime will become owned by a charitable trust that secures our continued independence.

Los Angeles | London | New Delhi | Singapore | Washington DC

4E

BASIC COUNSELLING SKILLS

A HELPER'S MANUAL

RICHARD NELSON-JONES

Los Angeles | London | New Delhi
Singapore | Washington DC

Los Angeles | London | New Delhi
Singapore | Washington DC

SAGE Publications Ltd
1 Oliver's Yard
55 City Road
London EC1Y 1SP

SAGE Publications Inc.
2455 Teller Road
Thousand Oaks, California 91320

SAGE Publications India Pvt Ltd
B 1/I 1 Mohan Cooperative Industrial Area
Mathura Road
New Delhi 110 044

SAGE Publications Asia-Pacific Pte Ltd
3 Church Street
#10-04 Samsung Hub
Singapore 049483

Editor: Susannah Trefgarne
Assistant editor: Laura Walmsley
Production editor: Rachel Burrows
Marketing manager: Tamara Navaratnam
Cover design: Lisa Harper-Wells
Typeset by: C&M Digitals (P) Ltd, Chennai, India

Library of Congress Control Number: 2014956137

British Library Cataloguing in Publication data

A catalogue record for this book is available from
the British Library

ISBN 978-1-4739-1298-4
ISBN 978-1-4739-1299-1 (pbk)

CONTENTS

LIST OF ACTIVITIES

ABOUT THE AUTHOR

Richard Nelson-Jones was born in London in 1936. Having spent five years in California as a Second World War refugee, he returned there in the 1960s to obtain a master's and PhD from Stanford University. In 1970, he was appointed at the University of Aston to establish a Diploma in Counselling in Educational Settings. During the 1970s, he was helped by three Fulbright Professors from the United States, each for a year. During this period he broadened from a predominantly client-centred orientation to become much more cognitive-behavioural. He also wrote numerous articles and the first edition, published in 1982, of what is now *Nelson-Jones' Theory and Practice of Counselling and Psychotherapy*. In addition, he chaired the British Psychological Society's Working Party on Counselling and, in 1982, became the first chairperson of the BPS Counselling Psychology Section.

In 1984, Richard took up a position as a counselling and later counselling psychology trainer at the Royal Melbourne Institute of Technology, where he became an Associate Professor. During the period 1984 to 1997, he trained hundreds of students. He continued writing professional and research articles, and also books which were published in London and Sydney. In 1997, Richard retired from RMIT and moved to Chiang Mai in Thailand. There, as well as doing some counselling and teaching, he has continued as an author of counselling and counselling psychology text-books. He now lives in Chiang Mai and London, and regularly spends time in Australia.

PREFACE

Welcome to the fourth edition of *Basic Counselling Skills: A Helper's Manual*. Those using counselling skills can be divided into two groups: professionally accredited counsellors/psychotherapists and helpers. Helpers are all those people who use counselling skills as paraprofessional or quasi-counsellors, as part of non-counselling primary work roles, as volunteers in counselling and helping agencies, or in peer support groups. The prime purpose of this book is to support the training and practice of such helpers. In addition, the book may be used as an introduction to counselling skills for those intending to become professional counsellors.

I designed the previous editions of the book in response to the question 'How can I make this book as easy to access and learn from as possible?' Again, in this fourth edition, I divide the book into 29 brief chapters or learning units and restrict myself to essential content only. I do not provide references throughout the text since this book is intended for a practitioner rather than for an academic audience.

The book is divided into three parts. *Part I, Introduction*, consists of six chapters that lay the groundwork for understanding the use of basic counselling skills across a range of settings. At the end of Chapters 3 to 6 there are activities designed to help readers get more involved. *Part II, Specific Counselling Skills*, consists of 17 chapters designed to introduce a wide range of basic counselling skills. Each chapter describes the skill, provides one or more examples of its use, and then encourages you to practise the skill by undertaking one or more activities. *Part III, Further Considerations*, consists of six chapters. The first two chapters introduce relaxation and how to manage crises. The remaining chapters aim to raise your awareness of ethical issues, dealing with clients from different backgrounds, supervision, and how to become more skilled. Again, each of these chapters ends with one or more activities. In addition, I provide an annotated bibliography and contact details of professional associations in the UK, Australia and America.

This preface is concise and to the point. I hope that you will find all 29 chapters of this book similarly focused. Good luck and good skills.

Richard Nelson-Jones

INTRODUCTION

WHO ARE COUNSELLORS AND HELPERS?

Below are concerns that people have.

'Nurse, I'm worried that I am not getting better quicker.'

'I'm finding it difficult to adjust to this country; it's very different from where I come from.'

'I would like to get on better with my wife before she leaves me.'

'I w-w-wish that I c-could get over my st-st-st-stut-tering.'

'I'm always concerned about how other people feel about me.'

'I want to be able to make friends more easily.'

'I want help to learn to control my temper more.'

'We're having trouble in our sex life.'

'I've been made redundant and don't know what I want to do next.'

'I feel depressed much of the time.'

'We're short of money and row all the time about it.'

'I'm being bullied.'

'I can't concentrate properly because of what is going on at home.'

'I get very anxious about exams.'

'I want to handle people who have trouble with my being of a different race, better.'

'I would like to get more in touch with my strengths and be more positive.'

'My husband died six months ago and I still can't get over it.'

There are at least six categories of people who might offer help with such concerns. First, there are professional counsellors and psychotherapists. Such counselling and therapy professionals, who have undergone training on appropriately accredited courses, include clinical psychologists, counsel-ling psychologists, psychotherapists, counsellors and some psychiatrists and social workers. Second, there are paraprofessional or quasi-counsellors, who may have considerable training in counselling, yet are not accredited as counselling professionals. Third, there are those who use counselling and helping skills as part of their work. Here the primary focus of the work may be teaching, managing, supervising, or providing religious, social work, medical, financial, legal and trade union services. These jobs require people to use counselling skills some of the time if they are to be maximally effective in them. Fourth, there are voluntary counsellors and helpers. Volunteers usually receive training in counselling skills. They may work in settings like youth counselling services and in numerous voluntary agen-cies that provide invaluable services, such as Samaritans. Fifth, there are people who are part of peer helping or support networks of varying degrees of formality. Such peer support networks frequently cover areas of diversity such as culture, race, sexual orientation, and support for women and for men. Sixth, there are informal helpers. All of us have the opportunity to assist others, be it in the role of marital partner, parent, friend, relative or work colleague.

In addition to counsellors and helpers, there are now coaches who focus on the needs of the less disturbed. For example, in 2002 the Association for Coaching and in 2005 the British Psychological Society's interest group in coaching psychology were established. More recently, in June 2010 the British Association for Counselling and Psychotherapy launched a coach-ing division. A distinction can be made between coaching as an approach to training less-disturbed populations in skills, and coaching involving instruction (speaking, demonstration and rehearsing) in assisting helpees and clients to develop a specific skill or skills. Nevertheless, counselling and coaching overlap, with counsellors and helpers needing coaching skills and coaches requiring counselling skills in their repertoires.

In the above paragraphs, as is still often the case in everyday parlance, I sometimes used the terms counsellors and helpers as though they are inter-changeable. However, this blurring is likely to become increasingly difficult to maintain as the counselling and psychotherapy profession becomes more established and regulated. I now clarify some differences between counsellors and helpers.

WHO ARE COUNSELLORS?

Here I group as counsellors all those who are professionally trained and accredited to conduct counselling and psychotherapy. Therapy is derived from the Greek work *therapeia*, meaning healing. Attempts to differentiate between counselling and psychotherapy are never wholly successful. Because counselling and psychotherapy represent diverse rather than uniform knowledge and activities, it is more helpful to think of counselling approaches and psychological or 'talking' therapies.

Possible ways of attempting to distinguish counselling from psychotherapy include: that psychotherapy deals more with mental disorders than counselling; that psychotherapy is longer-term and deeper; and that psychotherapy is predominantly associated with medical settings. However, matters are by no means this clear-cut. Many counsellors work in medical settings, have helpees with recognized mental disorders, and do longer-term work that may or may not be of a deep psychodynamic nature.

There is a huge overlap between counselling and psychotherapy. As an illustration of this overlap, the Psychotherapy and Counselling Federation of Australia promulgates 'A definition of counselling and psychotherapy' as a single statement. Both counselling and psychotherapy are psychological processes that use the same theoretical models. Each stresses the need to value the helpee as a person, to listen carefully and sympathetically to what they have to say, and to foster the capacity for self-help and personal responsibility. For the purposes of this book, the terms counselling and psychotherapy are used interchangeably. Box 1.1 profiles three examples of counselling and psychotherapy professionals.

BOX 1.1   EXAMPLES OF PROFESSIONAL COUNSELLORS AND PSYCHOTHERAPISTS

Amelia, 45, is an accredited counsellor in private practice who specializes in helpees with relationship problems, be they couples, individual partners, families or children. Since she has built trust in her ability with a number of local general practitioners, they refer helpees to her.

Oliver, 34, is a counselling psychologist at a large multinational company. Much of his time is spent working with employees whose performance is suffering because of emotional difficulties. People who are referred to Oliver include those who are under-performing when working on their own and those who are having difficulty relating to fellow staff and/or helpees.

Ava, 29, is an accredited student counsellor in a university setting. Though most of her helpees are students, she also sees some academic and non-academic staff. In addition Ava leads training groups in such areas as study skills, assertion skills, and managing conflict skills.

What constitutes professional training as a counsellor? Though subject to change, the following gives the reader some idea of what is required. Courses recognized by the British Association for Counselling and Psychotherapy (BACP) must deliver a minimum of 400 hours of staff/student contact time, with, in addition, students undertaking a minimum of 100 hours supervised counselling practice. Such courses are likely to have a minimum duration of at least one year full-time study or two, three or four years' part-time study. For those wishing to train as psychotherapists, training offered by organizational members of the United Kingdom Council for Psychotherapy (UKCP) is not normally shorter than four years' part-time duration. Such training involves supervised clinical work and usually personal therapy in the model being taught. In Australia, the Psychotherapy and Counselling Federation of Australia (PACFA) requires Postgraduate Equivalent courses run by its member associations, over a minimum of two years, to consist of 200 hours of person-to-person training and 50 hours of supervision relating to 200 hours of helpee contact.

Regarding professional qualifications, two further points are worthy of mention. First, a number of people, such as some social workers and nurses, combine professional qualifications in their primary role with professional qualifications in counselling and psychotherapy. Second, completion of an approved course of counselling or psychotherapy training can no longer be equated with accreditation, since increasingly, professional counsellors and psychotherapists are required to undertake mandatory continuing professional development (CPD) requirements by their professional associations.

WHO ARE HELPERS?

Sometimes, as in the case of Gerard Egan's textbook *The Skilled Helper*, the term helper is used as a generic term to cover all those engaged in using counselling and helping skills, be they counselling and psychotherapy professionals or otherwise. Here, I use the term helper in a more restricted sense to include paraprofessional or quasi-counsellors, those who use counselling skills as part of other primary roles, those engaged in voluntary counselling and helping, and those who participate in peer helping or support networks.

Paraprofessional counsellors are trained in counselling skills, but at a level that falls short of professional counselling or psychotherapy accreditation. For example, some nurses have attended a number of counselling courses and may be skilled at dealing with the problems of specific categories of patients. People with such backgrounds might be called counsellors in their work settings, for example nurse counsellors. However, if the term counsellor in a given context is limited only to those with recognized professional qualifications and accreditation in the area, paraprofessional counsellors become categorized as helpers, despite the quality of their counselling skills.

Box 1.2 provides some examples of helpers who might not be considered paraprofessional counsellors, yet are using counselling skills as part of their work, in voluntary settings, or on a peer support basis. The examples in Box 1.2 are only illustrative of the vast range of people who use counselling skills when performing helping roles.

BOX 1.2   EXAMPLES OF HELPERS USING COUNSELLING SKILLS

Emily, 54, works as a nurse in a large hospital. Emily uses counselling skills to assist patients to handle both their physical and emotional problems better. She also helps some patients talk about some of the problems they will face on going home.

Jack, 38, is a social worker in a poor urban setting. He uses counselling skills to help people talk about their problems, their finances, and also how they can get more out of their lives.

Pooja, 46, is a secondary school teacher who has taken some counselling skills courses. She uses counselling skills to help pupils deal better with their learning difficulties, personal problems and educational/occupational choice decisions.

Olivia, 28, is a speech therapist who uses counselling skills both to assist helpees to talk about their difficulties in speaking properly and then to support them as she trains them to speak better.

Harry, 22, meets regularly with Jacob, 21, as part of a gay persons' support group. Harry and Jacob engage in co-helping in which, whenever they meet, they share the time between them so that each has a turn to be in the helpee and helper roles.

Rajiv, 34, is a community and youth worker in a city where, in the last 50 years or so, a large number of migrants have come from south Asia. His job includes helping recent migrants adjust to a new culture, assisting parents and children to relate better, and helping young people to find meaningful activities and stay out of trouble. Rajiv also helps people to cope better with racist incidents.

Isla, 61, works at a pregnancy advice centre and uses counselling skills to help both women who want to increase their chances of having a healthy baby and also those who wish to terminate a pregnancy.

Let's take a further look at some ways in which helpers can be distinguished from professional counsellors and psychotherapists. So far two main distinguishing areas have been identified. Helpers perform different *roles* to those of counsellors and psychotherapists. Counsellors have as their primary role conducting counselling, whether this be individual, couple, group or family counselling. Helpers often either have their primary role in another area or are using helping skills in voluntary and peer support capacities. Related to different roles, helpers differ from counsellors in their *training*. Counsellors are primarily trained to counsel, whereas helpers may be primarily trained to be social workers, nurses, probation officers, priests, welfare workers, managers and a host of other occupations. Furthermore, voluntary workers usually have primary work roles in non-counselling occupations, for which they have likely received the bulk of their training.

The *goals* of helping can both overlap with, yet differ from, those of counselling. The primary purpose of counselling and psychotherapy is to aid helpees to address psychological issues in their lives, for example becoming less depressed or anxious, and to work through decisions and crises that have a distinct psychological dimension to them. Sometimes such psychological issues are central to helping. On other occasions, helpers use counselling skills to assist people to deal with goals where the overt psychological dimensions appear secondary, if not irrelevant, to the recipients of the service, for instance, receiving pregnancy advice or probation and parole support.

The *settings* or contexts for helping can differ from those for counselling. Most often counselling takes place in offices, be they private or institutional, set aside specifically for that activity. The décor of such offices is designed to support the purpose of counselling, for instance, functional easy chairs with a coffee table between them. Often, counselling services are located in specially designated areas, such as student counselling services. Helpers may sometimes use counselling skills in areas designed for counselling, for instance, in some voluntary agencies. However, frequently helpers use counselling skills in locations that represent their primary work role. Such locations include personnel offices, classrooms, tutorial rooms, hospital wards, outplacement clinics, churches, banks, law offices and community centres. Furthermore, while counsellors rarely go outside formal locations, helpers such as priests, nurses, social workers and members of peer support networks may use counselling skills in people's home settings.

A further distinction is that often the *relationship* in which helpers use counselling skills often differs from the more formal counselling relationship, which is likely to have clear boundaries structured around the respective tasks of counsellor and helpee. Sometimes helping relationships may have similarly clear helper–helpee boundaries, though the prime agenda may or may not be psychological counselling. Frequently, however, helping relationships take place in the context of other relationships, such as teacher–student, priest–parishioner, line manager–worker, social worker–client, and nurse– or doctor–patient. Whereas dual relationships, in which counsellors perform more than one role in relation to helpees, are frowned upon in counselling, they may be built into the fabric of many helping relationships. Furthermore, as mentioned above, sometimes helping relationships include home visits.

HELPERS AND HELPEES

For the purposes of this book, the term **helper** is used to refer to all those people who use counselling skills as paraprofessional or quasi-counsellors, as part of non-counselling primary work roles, as volunteers in counselling and helping agencies, or in peer support networks. Though some such helpers might nevertheless be called counsellors, the term counsellor in this book is reserved for professionally trained and accredited counsellors and psychotherapists.

The term **helpee** is used as a shorthand way to describe the numerous people with whom helpers interact when they use counselling skills. Some such people may already be referred to as clients. However, just as helpers may not have their primary role as counsellors, helpees too may have other primary roles such as pupils, students, customers, patients, local residents, young people, old people and peers.

WHAT ARE BASIC COUNSELLING SKILLS?

CHAPTER GOALS

By studying this chapter you should:

- Understand what communication and action skills are.
- Be introduced to what mind skills are.
- Understand about feelings and physical reactions.

This chapter introduces the idea of basic or fundamental counselling skills. What is a counselling skill? One application of the word skills pertains to *areas* of skill, for instance, listening skills or disclosing skills. Another application refers to *level of competence*, for instance, how strong your skills are in a particular area. Competence in a skill is best viewed not as an either/or matter in which you either possess or do not possess a skill. Rather, within a skills area, it is preferable to think of possessing different levels of strength. In all skills areas you are likely to possess a mixture of levels of strength. For instance, in the skills area of listening, you may be stronger at understanding helpees, but less strong at showing your understanding. Similarly, in just about all areas of their functioning, helpees possess a mixture of skills of differing levels of strength.

A third application of the word skill relates to the *knowledge and sequence of choices* entailed in implementing a given skill. The essential element of any skill is the ability to make and implement sequences of choices to achieve objectives. For instance, if you are to be good at listening deeply and accurately to helpees, you have to make and implement effective choices in this skills area. The object of counselling skills training and supervision is to help trainee helpers, in the skills areas targeted by their training programmes, move more in the direction of making choices that reflect strength. For example, in the skills area of active listening the objective would be to enable you to make stronger choices in the process not only of understanding clients but also in showing that understanding to them.

When thinking of any area of helper or helpee communication, there are two main considerations: first, what are the components of skilled external behaviour and, second, what interferes with or enhances enacting that behaviour? Thus, a counselling skill like active listening consists both of skilled interpersonal communication and skilled intrapersonal mental processing. One approach to understanding this is to acknowledge that outer behaviour originates in the mind and that, as a consequence, both thinking and behaviour are fundamentally mental processes. However, here I distinguish between two main categories of helper and helpee skills. First, there are communication and action skills, or skills that entail external behaviour. Second, there are mind skills, or skills that entail internal behaviour. You may wonder why I do not talk about feelings skills and physical reactions skills. The reason for this is that feelings and physical reactions are essentially part of your instinctual or animal nature and are not skills in themselves. However, as helpers and helpees you can influence how you feel and physically react by how you communicate/act and think.

COMMUNICATION AND ACTION SKILLS

Communication and action skills involve observable behaviours. They are what you do and how you do it rather than what and how you feel and think. For instance, it is one thing for you to feel concern for helpees, and another to act on this feeling. How do you communicate to helpees and act to show sympathy and compassion for them? You need to do so with your words, voice and body language. Communication and action skills vary by area of application, for instance, listening skills, questioning skills and challenging skills. Box 2.1 presents the five main ways in which helpers and helpees can send communication and action skills messages.

BOX 2.1   FIVE MAIN WAYS OF SENDING COMMUNICATION/ ACTION SKILLS MESSAGES

Verbal messages   Messages sent with words.

Vocal messages   Messages sent through your voice: for example, through volume, articulation, pitch, emphasis and speech rate.

Body messages   Messages sent from your body: for instance, through gaze, eye contact, facial expression, posture, gestures, physical proximity, and clothes and grooming.

Touch messages   A special category of body messages; messages sent with touch through the parts of the body that you use, what parts of another's body you touch, how gentle or firm you are, and whether or not you have permission.

Taking action messages   Messages sent when not face-to-face, for example, sending letters, e-mails or invoices.

MIND SKILLS

In the last 60 years or so, there has been a major trend in counselling and psychotherapy towards trying to change helpees' self-defeating thoughts and mental processes as a way of assisting them to feel and act better. These approaches are known as the cognitive therapies. The same insights can be applied to your thoughts and mental processes as you both learn and use counselling skills.

You can learn counselling skills and assist helpees much more effectively if you harness your mind's potential. How can you control your thoughts so that you can beneficially influence how you communicate? First, you can understand that you have a mind with a capacity for meta-cognitive thinking – thinking about thinking – that you can develop. Second, you can become much more efficient in thinking about your thinking if you view your mental processes in terms of skills that you can train yourself to exercise and control. Third, in daily life as well as in counselling skills training, you can assiduously practise using your mind skills to influence your communication.

Counselling skills involve mental processing both to guide external behaviour and to ensure thinking that supports rather than undermines skilled external communication. Let's take the skill of active listening. To some extent it is easy to describe the central elements of the external communication involved. On paper, these external communication skills may appear straightforward. However, most counselling skills trainees and many experienced counsellors and helpers struggle to listen well. The question then arises: 'If the external communication skills of listening well are so relatively easy to outline, why don't trainees and experienced helpers just do them?' The simple answer is that your mind can both enhance and get in the way of your external communication. Thus, counselling skills consist of both mind and communication skills.

Box 2.2 provides descriptions of three central mental processes or mind skills. These skills are derived from the work of leading cognitive therapists, such as Aaron Beck and Albert Ellis. These mind skills are relevant to clients and you alike. The contents of Chapters 18, 19 and 20 of this book, focusing on strategies for changing clients' thinking in these mind skills areas, also apply to changing your thinking.

BOX 2.2   THREE CENTRAL MIND SKILLS

Creating self-talk   Instead of talking to yourself negatively before, during and after specific situations, you can acknowledge that you have choices and make coping self-statements that assist you to stay calm and cool, establish your goals, coach yourself in what to do, and affirm your strengths, skills and support factors. In addition, you can use self-talk to create visual images that support verbal self-statements.

Creating rules Your unrealistic rules make irrational demands on you, others and the environment: for instance, 'I must always be happy', 'Others must look after me' and 'My environment should not contain any suffering'. Instead you can develop realistic or preferential rules, for instance, 'I prefer to be happy much of the time, but it is unrealistic to expect this all the time.'

Creating perceptions You can learn to test the reality of your perceptions rather than jump to conclusions. You can distinguish between fact and inference and make your inferences as accurate as possible.

In reality, mind skills tend to overlap. For instance, all of the skills involve self-talk. However, here self-talk refers to self-statements relevant to coping with specific situations. Interrelationships between skills can also be viewed on the dimension of depth. Arguably, helpers or helpees who believe in the rule 'I must always be happy' are more prone to perceiving events as negative than those who do not share this rule.

FEELINGS AND PHYSICAL REACTIONS

To a large extent, you are what you feel. Important feelings include happiness, interest, surprise, fear, sadness, anger and disgust or contempt. Dictionary definitions of feelings tend to use words like 'physical sensation', 'emotions' and 'awareness'. All three of these words illustrate a dimension of feelings. Feelings as *physical sensations* or as *physical reactions* represent your underlying animal nature. People are animals first, persons second. As such you need to learn to value and live with your underlying animal nature. The word *emotions* implies movement. Feelings are processes. You are subject to a continuous flow of biological experiencing. *Awareness* implies that you can be conscious of your feelings. However, at varying levels and in different ways, you may also be out of touch with them.

Physical reactions both represent and accompany feelings and, in a sense, are indistinguishable. For example, bodily changes associated with anxiety can include galvanic skin response (detectable electrical changes taking place in the skin), raised blood pressure, a pounding heart and a rapid pulse, shallow and rapid breathing, muscular tension, drying of the mouth, stomach problems such as ulcers, speech difficulties such as stammering, sleep difficulties, and sexual problems such as complete or partial loss of desire. Other physical reactions include a slowing-down of body movements when depressed and dilated eye pupils in moments of anger or sexual attraction.

Sometimes you react to your physical reactions. For example, in anxiety and panic attacks, you may first feel tense and anxious and then become even more tense and anxious because of this initial feeling.

Feelings and physical reactions are central to the helping process. You require the capacity to experience and understand both your own and helpees' feelings. However, just because feelings represent your animal nature, this does not mean that you and your helpees cannot act on them. In helping, there are three somewhat overlapping areas where feelings and accompanying physical reactions are important: experiencing feelings, expressing feelings and managing feelings. In each of these three areas, you can work with helpees' communications/actions and thoughts and mental processes to influence how they feel and physically react.

BASIC COUNSELLING SKILLS

Let's get down to basics. The word basic, when used in conjunction with counselling skills, implies a repertoire of counselling skills on which you can base your helping practice. Such skills are fundamental or primary rather than advanced. The quality of the helper–helpee relationship is essential to successful helping encounters. Consequently, many basic skills are those that will enhance how well you and helpees connect. Such skills include understanding the helpees' internal frames of reference or points of view and reflecting their feelings. Other basic skills entail assisting helpees to understand their problems and situations more clearly; for example, you can ask key questions about feelings, physical reactions, thoughts, communications and actions. Still other basic skills can focus on simple and straightforward ways of assisting helpees to change how they think, feel, communicate and act. All helpers require basic counselling skills for relating to helpees and for assisting them to understand their concerns. The extent and ways in which you extend your repertoire of basic counselling skills to include skills for assisting helpee change are likely to be a matter of what each of you finds useful.

HELPERS AND HELPEES AS DIVERSE PERSONS

By studying and doing the activity in this chapter you should:

- Know more about different characteristics that helpers and helpees bring to helping.
- Become aware of how these characteristics might influence helping.

Over the past 45 years or so there has been a growing interest in diversity-sensitive counselling and helping. Apart from personal histories, all helpers and helpees possess a mixture of different characteristics. You also possess perceptions and evaluations of these different characteristics in yourselves and others. There is no such thing as perfect helper–helpee matching, though there may be important and often desirable similarities, for example, regarding culture or race. Box 3.1 indicates just some of the many areas of diversity in the practice of counselling and helping. I briefly discuss each of these areas in turn.

BOX 3.1 TEN AREAS OF DIVERSITY IN COUNSELLING AND HELPING

1 **Culture** Ancestral origins in either the mainstream or in a minority group culture and, if the latter, degree of acculturation.
2 **Race** Possessing distinctive physical characteristics according to a racial sub-grouping or being of mixed race.
3 **Social class** Differences attached to such matters as income, educational attainment and occupational status.
4 **Biological sex** Female or male.
5 **Gender-role identity** Differences in feelings, thoughts and behaviour according to the social classification of attributes as 'feminine' or 'masculine'.

(Continued)

(Continued)

6 **Marital status**   Single, cohabiting, married, separated, divorced, remarried or widowed.
7 **Sexual and affectionate orientation**   Heterosexual, lesbian, gay or bisexual.
8 **Age**   Childhood, adolescence, young adulthood, middle age, late middle age or old age.
9 **Physical disability**   A deficiency in the structure or functioning of some part or parts of the body.
10 **Religion or philosophy**   Christian, Hindu, Muslim, Buddhist or some other religious or secular belief system.

CULTURE

In mid-2014, the total population of the United Kingdom numbered 64.6 million people, up from 58.8 million people in the 2001 census. The 2011 census showed that, for England and Wales, 46 per cent or 3.4 million identified with a White ethnic group. Among these was a large increase in the number of people of Polish origin. Thirty-three per cent or 2.4 million identified as Asian/Asian British, and 13 per cent or 922,000 identified with the Black/African/Caribbean/Black British group.

Australia's population has grown more than sixfold since the beginning of the twentieth century, from 3.8 million to 22.8 million in 2012. Australia has changed from being a predominantly British-based culture to one of the most multicultural and increasingly multiracial countries in the world. For some years now Asians have been the largest migrant group.

The United States of America has a long history of cultural diversity. In 2010 the US population was 308.7 million. The majority were still white (63.7 per cent white-non-Hispanic), with their ancestry in numerous countries. Of the remainder, 16.2 per cent were white-Hispanic or Latino in origin, 12.6 black or African American, and 4.6 Asian.

Helpers and helpees can come from different cultures and be at differing levels of assimilation to the mainstream culture. Even if you both come from the mainstream culture you may have differing levels of adaptation or rejection of its main rules and conventions. Helpers and helpees who are native-born of migrant parents may experience split loyalties between the pull of parental cultures and personal wishes to assimilate into mainstream culture.

Helpers and helpees who are migrants may experience differing levels of repulsion and attraction to both your previous and new home cultures. Migrants always carry around part of previous cultures in their hearts and heads. Some migrants are never really happy in their host countries.

However, migrants idealizing previous cultures can get a rude awakening when going home for the first time.

In addition to the cultures that helpers and helpees bring, you each have differing experiences of how accepted you have been within your own and other cultures. Some will have been fortunate enough to have cultural differences accepted and cherished, while others will have received feedback that their cultures are inferior.

An important cultural issue relates to expectations about helper and helpee roles. For example, cultures may differ in their rules about whom they consider appropriate help givers, the appropriateness of disclosing personal information to strangers, how they exhibit different emotions and symptoms, and the degree of direction expected from helpers. In addition, cultures differ in their attitude to time and to the making and keeping of appointments.

RACE

You and your helpees may come from different races. Whereas cultural differences can be subtle, racial differences are readily observable. Also, both you and your helpees may have experienced or be experiencing racial discrimination in relation to the majority white host culture. Sometimes those from majority cultures can feel suspicion and hostility when venturing into minority cultures. The idea of racially matching helpers and helpees (black with black, Asian with Asian, etc.) is not universally supported. However, many relationships between helpers and helpees who are of different races involve working through and moving beyond racial stereotypes. It is important to possess race-sensitive as well as culture-sensitive skills: for instance, some helpees may appreciate permission to share their views on the role of race in their lives and in the helping relationship.

SOCIAL CLASS

Social class is still a big issue in the UK and, possibly to a lesser extent, in Australia and the United States. Income, educational attainment and occupational status are currently three of the main measures of social class in Western countries. Other indicators include schooling, accent, clothing, manners, nature of social networks, and type and location of housing.

You and your helpees bring social class into your relationships. You also bring your sensitivity to the effects of others' social class on you, and your social class on others. If insufficiently skilled, social class considerations may create unnecessary barriers to establishing effective helping relationships.

If you possess feelings of either inferiority or superiority on account of your social class, you should strive to eliminate them. Being an effective helper is difficult enough without the intrusion of avoidable social class agendas.

BIOLOGICAL SEX

You and your helpees bring your biological sex to your relationship. In most formal counselling settings, women outnumber men both as helpers and helpees. This is less likely to be the case in settings where helpers are using counselling skills as part of other primary roles. In such instances the sex ratio of helpers and helpees may be more likely to reflect that of the working context, be it educational, health or business. Whether the helping relationship exists between people of the same sex or of different sexes will likely influence the quantity and quality of the communication within it, but this may be for better or worse depending on those involved.

GENDER-ROLE IDENTITY

As well as sometimes referring to biological sex, gender also refers to the social and cultural classification of attributes and behaviours as 'masculine' and 'feminine'. You and your helpees bring your gender or sex-role identities to the relationship – how you view yourselves and one another on the dimensions of 'masculinity' and 'femininity' and the importance you attach to these constructs.

You and your helpees can be categorized according to the importance you attach to gender issues, for instance, to what extent and in what ways you are advocates for women's or men's issues. Furthermore, both parties may vary in the extent to which you possess sexist views that assume the superiority of one sex over the other: for instance, in attitudes to the roles of men and women in the workforce, sexual harassment, and domestic psychological and physical violence.

MARITAL STATUS

Though predominant among younger people, there is a trend towards people cohabiting outside of marriage. Nevertheless most adults in Western countries still end up getting married. However, people appear to be marrying later. For instance, in England and Wales, only 16 per cent of men who married in 2000 were aged under 25, compared with 38 per cent in 1990, with the corresponding proportions for single women being 30 and 57 per cent respectively. Divorce is also becoming more common. In mid-2000 the proportion of divorced people in England and Wales was 9.1 per cent compared with 5.0 per cent in 1990. In most instances where helpers use counselling skills as part of other primary roles, your marital status is likely to be considered irrelevant by yourself and by your helpees. However, when you assist helpees in improving intimate relationships, your marital status might be an issue for some of them.

SEXUAL AND AFFECTIONATE ORIENTATION

You and your helpees bring your sexual orientation to the helping relationship, whether you are heterosexual, lesbian, gay or bisexual. I use the term sexual orientation rather than sexual preference. Many, if not most, predominantly lesbian and gay people's sexual orientation is a fact of life, based on genetics and significant learning experiences, rather than a preference, based on free choice. Sometimes the term affectionate orientation is now used as a way of acknowledging that in same-sex relationships, as in opposite-sex ones, there are many other aspects than the sexual.

You and your helpees not only bring your sexual and affectionate orientation to helping relationships; you bring your thoughts and feelings about your own and other people's sexual orientation too. Lesbian, gay and bisexual helpers and helpees may be at varying levels of acceptance of your own or other people's homosexuality. Each of you may need to cope with stigmatization, family rejection, oppression, sexual identity issues, and internalized societal homophobia. Lesbian and gay helpees may wonder about the sexual orientation and attitudes of helpers and fear that helpers will have difficulty accepting them.

Probably few helpers are openly homophobic, but many may, in varying degrees, be heterosexist. By heterosexist, I mean that either knowingly or unknowingly you assume the superiority of demonstrating affection towards members of the opposite sex. On the other hand, some lesbian and gay helpers may have difficulty working with repressed heterosexuality or the openly heterosexual components of bisexual clients. Wittingly or unwittingly, you may seek to influence such clients into lesbian and gay moulds.

AGE

Immediately you and your helpees meet for the first time, you start making assumptions about, and connected with, one another's age. Assessment of age may be the starting point for other thoughts and feelings about yourselves and one another. For example, young helpers may perceive yourselves as being out of your depth with older helpees since you do not have sufficient life experience. Young helpees may fear that older helpers will be unable to understand them on account of the generation gap.

One aspect of age that is changing is life expectancy; for instance, on average, Western people are living some 20 years or more than a century ago. This change has many challenges for helping, including paying more attention to the needs of older people. Age is partly a physical concept, but it is also an attitude of mind. Older people can be psychologically alive and vibrant, whereas some young people are mentally rigid. Also, how helpers and helpees communicate can reinforce or dispel assumptions based on physical age. For example, youthful helpers can communicate in calm and comfortable ways that reassure older helpees, while older helpers can show understanding of young helpees' culture and aspirations.

PHYSICAL DISABILITY

Either you or your helpee, or both of you, may be physically disabled in some way. Many people suffer from mobility, hearing, sight and other impairments. Sometimes these impairments are genetic and on other occasions result from life events, such as industrial or car accidents or military service. You and your helpees will also have thoughts and feelings about your own or one another's disabilities. Some of you may rightly feel inadequately skilled to work with certain physically disabled helpees.

Being a physically disabled helper raises many issues. All physically disabled people have to come to terms with their physical restrictions. Many physically disabled helpers have become calmer and stronger people, having successfully navigated the emotional ramifications of disabilities. In addition to having added insights into the challenges faced by physically disabled helpees, such disabled people can be very effective helpers for the non-physically disabled.

Sometimes you may be under pressure to change the nature of the helping relationship because of other agendas connected with disabled helpees: for example, pressure from insurers' or workers' compensation boards for brief helping or to write reports about helpees. Though very much a minority, some disabled helpees may allow financial claim considerations to sabotage the integrity of helping relationships.

RELIGION OR PHILOSOPHY

You and your helpees bring religious beliefs, spiritual yearnings and explanations of the meaning of life to relationships. Such beliefs can be sources of strength. For example, in Western cultures, many helpers are strongly motivated by the Christian concept of *agape* or unselfish love. Furthermore, sharing the same religious beliefs as helpees can strengthen a collaborative working relationship. However, in some instances helpees may find their own, and possibly their helper's, religious beliefs unduly restrictive.

Helpers differ in ability to develop relationships with helpees whose attitudes towards religion and spirituality differ from their own. An issue for many religious helpers is the extent to which the values and teachings of your religion influence how you work. For instance, Roman Catholic helpers may face value conflicts with helpees in areas such as divorce, contraception, abortion and premarital or lesbian and gay sex.

Above I have reviewed 10 key characteristics that helpers and helpees bring to helping contacts and relationships. Personal characteristics come in different permutations and combinations. No helping relationship exists in a vacuum. You require sensitivity to the effect that your own and your helpees' personal characteristics have on how you communicate and on how you can best develop the helping relationship. You also need to be realistic about your limitations and be prepared to refer certain helpees to other helpers who might understand their special circumstances better.

INTRODUCTION TO ACTIVITIES

This chapter and all the other chapters in this book end with an activity or activities to help you to develop your knowledge and skills. Though my assumption is that you are learning basic counselling skills in training groups, this may not always be the case. Nevertheless, you may still want to perform some or all of the activities either with a partner or, if this is inconvenient, on your own. You will enhance the value of this book if you undertake the activities diligently. While practice may not make perfect, it can increase competence.

Trainers and trainees can decide how to proceed with each activity: for instance, whether the activity should be done as a whole group exercise, in threes, pairs, individually or using any combination of these approaches. When doing the activities, all concerned should ensure that no one feels under pressure to reveal any personal information that she or he does not want to. To save repetition, I only mention these instructions once here and not at the start of each activity.

Activity 3.1 Raising awareness of your own and helpees' different characteristics and their effects

1 How would you describe yourself on each of the following characteristics?

- culture
- race
- social class
- biological sex
- gender-role identity
- marital status
- sexual and affectionate orientation
- age
- physical disability
- religion or philosophy.

2 How do you think you might treat helpees who differ from you on any of the above characteristics, in ways that might interfere with helping? What can you do about each one?

WHAT YOU BRING TO COUNSELLING AND HELPING

4

By studying and doing the activities in this chapter you should:

- Explore your motives for being a helper.
- Start assessing how you experience feelings when helping.
- Start assessing your use of communication skills and mind skills when helping.

As well as the diverse characteristics described in the previous chapter, you also bring along many personal characteristics and levels of skill to learning about counselling and helping. Some of you may not be ready to have roles where you help others. You may need to work through personal problems before you can devote sufficient attention to deal with others in ways that are not too affected by your own needs. All trainee helpers bring various levels of strength in the component skills of being an effective helper. This chapter examines some of the skills and issues that you bring and should be mindful of during your training.

YOUR MOTIVES

Many of you want to help others because of deprivations in your pasts. For instance, you may feel that your parents did not give you enough love and support. Some of you may acknowledge that you grew up in circumstances where it was difficult to learn how to relate well to others and that you still have much learning to do. In varying degrees, others may not realize that you still need to acquire and strengthen your skills of relating to and respecting people who are different from you. You risk damaging your helpees if you cannot see them more objectively; for example, you may pressurize them in various ways to be dependent on you.

You need to be conscious of your motives for helping. It could even be an advantage having suffered some emotional pain and deprivation in the past, so long as you are aware of it and are prepared to work to become a stronger person. Because you have suffered in the past, you want to learn to help others who are suffering now. Some people are naturally inclined to want to help others and feel more fulfilled when doing so. Some may be influenced by religious beliefs to help others – for instance, if you are a Christian you want to show *agape* or selfless love. Each of you has your own array of motivations for wanting to help others.

You may seek to develop a career in helping and make a living from doing so. That is fine so long as you genuinely want to help others, work hard to develop your skills, and monitor your effectiveness. Even if neither working nor intending to work full-time as a helper, you may still be one of many wanting to help, either part-time or along with other roles, to strengthen people and lessen their suffering.

YOUR FEELINGS

As mentioned in Chapter 2, three important areas regarding feelings for helpers and helpees are experiencing feelings, expressing feelings and managing feelings. You bring your skills in each of these areas to your helping work.

EXPERIENCING FEELINGS

To be an effective helper you need to be able to experience your feelings fully and accurately. Let's take some examples of helping trainees unable or only partially able to experience feelings.

Case studies

Sanjay, 34, grew up in a home where both parents had difficulty in experiencing and openly showing their feelings. Consequently, Sanjay now has trouble experiencing what he really feels. Instead, he comes over as someone who is emotionally flat.

Jessica, 27, is able to experience some of her feelings – for instance, happiness and appreciation. However, she represses sexual feelings. She is very prim and proper and keeps men at a distance.

Jacob, 47, feels angry and loses his temper far too easily. Though he has many positive feelings towards those to whom he is close, he does not experience such feelings once he starts becoming angry.

In each of the above examples, the helping trainees need to work on being able to experience their feelings. By being able to relate to yourself through experiencing your feelings, this helps you to understand and relate more fully to different kinds of people who will be your helpees.

EXPRESSING FEELINGS

Helping trainees need to be able to express their feelings appropriately in daily life as well as in helping. Expressing your feelings is sometimes different when you are a helper than in daily life – for instance, you always have to consider the effect that this will have on helpees. Nevertheless, if as a helping trainee you are not strong at expressing your feelings in your daily life, you may also find difficulty appropriately expressing them to helpees.

Case studies

Poppy, 36, can generally experience what she feels. However, often she is inhibited about letting other people know what she feels. For instance, she is really pleased to have done so well in a recent examination, yet is reluctant to share her pleasure with her friends.

Charlie, 24, has a problem with expressing his feelings in that often other people feel overwhelmed by the aggressive way he does so. Then, when they do not respond as he would like, he tends to get even more aggressive.

Poppy and Charlie are two people who have difficulty expressing their feelings assertively in daily life. Such people are also more likely to find difficulty expressing their feelings appropriately as helpers. Becoming more assertive is covered later on in this chapter.

MANAGING FEELINGS

World-famous psychiatrist and author Irvin Yalom admits to having had difficulty managing feelings of disgust when faced with fat lady helpees. He needed to work on managing such feelings so that they did not get in the way of his effectiveness. In your daily life as well as your work as a helper, you may need to manage certain feelings so that you can then decide if, when and how to express them.

Case studies

Isabella, 32, was sexually abused by her father when growing up. Now she works as a helper in a centre that deals with many victims of sexual abuse. Isabella has had to work through her own reactions to being sexually abused, so that she can manage her feelings when dealing with helpees who have been or are being abused.

(Continued)

(Continued)

Yasmin, 21, sometimes lets her feelings about what other people are saying and how they are saying it get in the way of her really listening to them. She needs to identify situations when she is at risk of not listening properly and then manage her feelings so that she really listens.

Thomas, 28, lets himself be unduly influenced by people who pour out their troubles to him. He needs to learn to manage his feelings so that he can be genuinely helpful to them, instead of sometimes letting them manipulate him into just agreeing that they have been hard done by.

Can you think of situations in your life where you have difficulty managing your feelings? If so, you have taken the first step in learning how to manage them better.

SENSE OF WORTH

You bring your sense of worth to your work as a helper. Ideally, you should feel yourself a worthwhile or a realistically confident person. However, some people want to help others because they do not feel worthwhile themselves. If so, you may need to work on helping yourself to become more confident before you can help others properly. Most of you, while not being badly under-confident, could still have a higher sense of worth. Your feelings of insecurity may get in the way of your handling certain situations or awkward helpees as well as necessary. As you become a better helper, you should feel more confident. However, you may still need to learn to become more confident outside your helping roles, so that you can feel, think and act more confidently within them.

FEARS AND ANXIETIES

Related to your sense of worth are the amount and nature of your fears and anxieties. For instance, if you feel generally under-confident, you may well be afraid of not being as competent as you would like when helping, be it full-time or part-time. You may be anxious about dealing with specific kinds of people, for instance aggressive, shy or racially different helpees. You may have fears about helping helpees manage certain kinds of problems, for instance sexual or marital conflict ones. You may also have fears not directly connected with your helping work, but which, nevertheless, may cause you to be a less confident person in it. Such fears and anxieties include speaking in public, high places, criticism, being teased and being alone.

YOUR COMMUNICATION SKILLS

How well do you listen? Listening accurately and showing that you have heard them is central to helping others. In many ways, you can hinder others from communicating what they really think and feel. Let's start with the physical aspect of listening. Various ways in which you can make it difficult for people to talk with you include: being insufficiently available, staring, looking away, slouching, being either too far or too close, making the wrong gestures and dressing inappropriately, amongst others. Non-physical ways of not listening properly can include: talking too much, talking about yourself rather than tuning in to them, asking too many questions, interrupting, and being too quick to make judgements.

Listening well to another person is only partly about receiving their messages accurately. Even if you receive them accurately, you still need to let the other person know that you have done so. Therefore you need to send messages that show that you have heard them properly. Many of these messages will be verbal so you require good verbal skills that help others to feel understood. However, you also need to send good vocal messages to partners, colleagues and friends as well as to clients. You can go a long way to counteracting a good verbal message if you send poor vocal messages: for instance speaking too quietly, too emphatically, not clearly enough, or either too quickly or too slowly.

I will leave further discussion of these skills until later. Suffice it to say, most of us have never been consciously taught the skills of listening properly to others and communicating back that we have accurately heard. Those fortunate may have learned from good models, for instance parents and teachers, but most of us could still listen better. Also, the kind of listening and communicating in helping situations differs from that in most real-life situations in that the focus is more on helpees rather than on both of you.

YOUR MIND SKILLS

In Chapter 2, I introduced the notion of mind skills. While I focus on helping helpees develop their mind skills later on in the book, here I want to focus on the idea that you too might improve your mind skills. Perhaps it is best to start by getting you thinking in terms of mind skills rather than just thinking that you have thoughts. The notion of mind skills gives you a language for thinking effectively or skilfully about how you think. Once you have identified certain central mind skills, you then can start thinking about your thinking in these specific skills areas. For instance, you can start identifying how skilled you are in these areas and where you might improve. Next, you can work in various ways to think more skilfully.

Here are a few examples of helping students who might strengthen their mind skills.

Case studies

Creating self-talk   Sophie, 22, talks to herself very negatively before and during taking tests. Before taking them she gets herself anxious by telling herself she is going to fail and imagining doing so. During tests, she puts unnecessary pressure on herself by inwardly saying that she does not have enough time to do herself justice. Instead, Sophie needs to learn to tell herself repeatedly to stay calm and cool, that she can only do as well as she can, to think carefully about how much time to spend on each question, that she has strengths and skills, and lastly that there are people who will support her however well she does.

Creating rules   Oscar, 37, worries a lot about how well he is doing on his helping course. He thinks 'I must do everything perfectly' and 'The trainer and other students must see that I am a competent helper'. Oscar needs to become conscious of his perfectionist and demanding rules and then learn to dispute them and replace them with preferential rules: for instance, 'All I can do is do as well as I can' and 'While I might like the approval of the trainer and other students, what is more important is that I focus on building my helping skills'.

Creating perceptions   William, 41, perceives that he is doing poorly on his helping course. He needs to check the accuracy of this perception by asking questions like 'Where is the evidence?', 'Are there other ways of perceiving the situation?' and 'Which way of perceiving the situation best fits the available facts?' When William takes the trouble to ask himself these questions, he comes to the conclusion that the most accurate perception is: 'In actual fact I seem to be doing as well as the other students and we are all still learning to do even better.'

The mind skills that you will try to help helpees acquire and get stronger in are also skills that you require both in your daily life and in your helping training and work. Everyone needs to work not only on acquiring, but also on maintaining good mind skills. Helpers and helpees alike have areas in which they are more skilled and areas in which they could improve. However, usually helpees need to strengthen their mind skills more than their helpers do.

ASSERTIVENESS SKILLS

Beginning helpers often struggle with their ability to be assertive both in their daily lives and in their helping roles. Some trainee helpers are non-assertive in their daily lives and their helping work.

Case study

James, 33, is a speech therapist who fails to impose much structure in his interviews with helpees. He allows them to take far too much control over how the time is spent. Also, in his daily life James often does what other people want, even when he does not really want to do it.

Some trainee helpers are unnecessarily aggressive, though these tend to be very much a minority.

Case study

Mia, 27, is a social worker. Sometimes when people try to tell her that they have a legitimate problem, she tells them abruptly that she does not have much time to listen.

Leading writers on assertiveness Robert Alberti and Michael Emmons observe that assertive behaviour enables people to stand up for themselves without undue anxiety, express honest feelings comfortably, and exercise personal rights without denying the right of others. Here is an example of assertiveness.

Case study

George, 37, is a trainee helper in a youth centre. When Alfie, 16, one of the boys at the centre, speaks to him aggressively, George does not reply in kind. Instead he quietly but firmly acknowledges what Alfie has said in an angry way. George then asks Alfie to explain further. If Alfie continues being aggressive, George tactfully lets him know how he experiences him and asks him to speak more calmly.

COMMUNICATING ASSERTIVELY

Assertive communication consists of verbal, vocal and body messages. Assertive verbal messages tend to be 'I' messages that accept responsibility for your thoughts, feelings and actions rather than 'You' messages: for example, 'I would like you to do this' rather than 'You should do this'. Also, say what you really mean. Assertive vocal messages include speaking reasonably loudly, clearly articulating your words, avoiding being shrill, emphasizing words that back up your assertive message, and speaking at a measured pace.

Assertive body messages include looking the other person directly in the eye when delivering your assertive message, having a genuine facial expression, and using deliberate and non-threatening hand and arm movements to help express yourself in a constructive fashion.

THINKING ASSERTIVELY

Assertive mind skills underlie assertive communication. Alberti and Emmons emphasize that right thinking about assertiveness is crucial in that thoughts, beliefs, attitudes and feelings set the stage for behaviour. Many people interfere with their effectiveness by using negative self-talk. Illustrative negative self-statements are 'I'm a failure', 'I'm going to stuff it up' and 'I'll only make matters worse'. You can counteract your negative self-talk with calming and coping self-talk. Your calming self-statements include 'Relax' and 'Take it easy'. Your coping self-talk relates to the situation: for instance, George, above, might say to himself 'Give him the opportunity to explain himself further, though stand up for yourself firmly, if and when necessary.'

You may have created rules that do not allow you to be assertive – for instance, 'I must be nice all the time'. Once you become aware that you possess such a rule, you can logically analyse how realistic it is and what its positive and negative consequences are for you. Then, you can restate it as a flexible rule that works better for you. For instance, 'I must be nice all the time' might become 'While I prefer to be nice, it is also important in relationships, in and out of helping, to set appropriate boundaries and to stand up for myself.'

You may create perceptions about yourself and others that interfere with your being assertive. For instance, you may negatively label yourself as 'domineering' or 'bossy'. Among adjectives attached to assertiveness by women are 'un-feminine', 'bitchy' and 'castrating'. Assertiveness also requires you to perceive others accurately. You may overreact or underreact because you see others as more vulnerable or stronger than they are in reality. You can question the evidence for your perceptions, for instance, 'Where is the evidence that I am being bossy?' Then you can generate and consider alternative perceptions and choose the perception that best fits the available facts.

DEVELOP YOURSELF

In your training and work as helpers, you may also learn to become stronger in some of the skills that you are assisting your helpees to develop. As you work through the chapters in this book focused on strengthening your helping skills, remember that the more you possess good communication skills and mind skills in your own life, the more likely you are to exhibit them in your helping work. I now provide some activities designed to help you to develop yourself.

Activity 4.1   My motives

1 What are your motives for being a helper?
2 Which of these motives do you consider as positive?
3 Which motives have the potential to interfere with your effectiveness as a helper? What can you do to change them?

Activity 4.2   My feelings

1 Assess my strengths and ways that I might be stronger in experiencing my feelings. Are there any particular feelings that I find difficulty experiencing? If so, what can I do to experience these feelings more fully?
2 Assess my strengths and ways that I might be stronger in expressing my feelings. Are there any particular feelings that I find difficulty expressing? If so, what can I do to express these feelings better?
3 Assess my strengths and ways that I might be stronger in managing my feelings. Are there any particular feelings that I find difficulty managing? If so, what can I do to manage these feelings better?
4 How worthwhile or confident a person do I feel? Is there anything that I can do or think to help myself to feel more worthwhile?
5 What are my main fears and anxieties? Can I think of any ways in which realistically I might lessen these?

Activity 4.3   My communication skills

1 Assess my strengths and ways that I might be stronger in my verbal communication. Are there any particular ways and/or areas in which I might improve my verbal communication?
2 Assess my strengths and ways that I might be stronger in my vocal communication. Are there any particular ways in which I might improve my vocal communication?
3 Assess my strengths and ways I might be stronger in my bodily communication. Are there any particular ways that I might improve my bodily communication?
4 Assess my strengths and areas in which I might improve my receiving other people's communication. Are there any ways and/or areas in which I could improve my receiving communication skills?

Activity 4.4   My mind skills

1 Assess my strengths and ways that I might be stronger in creating self-talk. If necessary, what can I do to improve?
2 Assess my strengths and ways that I might be stronger in creating rules. If necessary, what can I do to improve?
3 Assess my strengths and ways that I might be stronger in creating perceptions. If necessary, what can I do to improve?

Activity 4.5   My assertiveness skills

1 Assess my communication on the following dimensions:

- non-assertiveness
- aggressiveness
- assertiveness.

2 Assess each of my mind skills in regard to thinking assertively:

- creating self-talk
- creating rules
- creating perceptions.

3 If necessary, what steps can I take to think more assertively?
4 If necessary, what steps can I take to communicate more assertively?

THE HELPING RELATIONSHIP

CHAPTER GOALS

By studying and doing the activity in this chapter you should:

- Know about the core conditions of helping relationships.
- Understand why the core conditions are important.
- Understand about collaboration in helping relationships.

In Chapter 1 I mentioned that helping relationships often are not as formal and clearly structured as counselling and psychotherapy relationships. A reason for this is that many helpers are using counselling skills in the context of other relationships, for instance, social worker–client or supervisor–worker. The idea of weekly 45–50-minute counselling sessions conducted in offices set aside for this purpose scarcely applies to large numbers of contacts between helpers and helpees. Sometimes helpers employ counselling skills in fairly long sessions, say, when offering support after bereavements or when conducting employment appraisals. Often, however, helpers use counselling skills in contacts with helpees that are relatively brief, say 10 to 15 minutes, and intermittent, as the need arises. Furthermore, though some helping relationships take place in counselling rooms, many helpers use their counselling skills in offices, hospital wards, classrooms, tutorial rooms, living rooms and factory canteen settings, among other locations. Consequently, you need to adapt the following discussion of helping relationships to the contexts in which you either use or will be using counselling skills.

DIMENSIONS OF HELPING RELATIONSHIPS

Connection is the essential characteristic of any relationship. Helping relationships are the human connections between helpers and helpees both in your direct dealings and in one another's heads. Within the overall relationship between helper and helpee, there are a number of dimensions or strands.

The public or observable relationship consists of all the communications relevant to any particular helper–helpee relationship. During helping contacts, both helper and helpee send and receive numerous verbal, vocal and body messages. In addition, helpers may provide helpees with written material, use a whiteboard, and sometimes make audio or video recordings. After helping, there may be further face-to face contact and, during or after helping, contact by phone, letter or e-mail.

Helping relationships take place in both participants' minds as well as in external communication. Many helpers and helpees have working relationships that precede or accompany helping relationships and, consequently, they have already started forming impressions of one another. During face-to-face helping, both participants relate to one another in their minds; for example, helpees may be deciding how far to trust helpers, how much to reveal, when and in what ways. In addition, both participants are constantly forming and re-forming mental conceptions of one another. Furthermore, in the periods between helping sessions and contacts, helpers and helpees engage in a mental relationship when thinking about one another and when reviewing material discussed together.

CORE CONDITIONS OF HELPING RELATIONSHIPS

In 1957, Carl Rogers published a seminal article entitled 'The necessary and sufficient conditions of therapeutic personality change'. In this article, Rogers identified six conditions for therapeutic change, three of which – empathic understanding, unconditional positive regard and congruence – are often referred to as the core conditions of helping relationships. In this book, I do not use the terms empathic understanding, unconditional positive regard and congruence, but use different terms to break down the counselling skills covered by these concepts. However, here I briefly describe each of the core conditions for two main reasons. First, the concepts provide valuable insights into how to strengthen rather than interfere with developing collaborative working relationships with helpees. Second, the terms empathy, unconditional regard and congruence are in such common use in the helping professions that readers should know what they mean. A final point is that British writers Dave Mearns and Mick Cooper have extended the core conditions by developing the concept of relational depth in which the encounter between helper and helpee, rather than the provision of a particular set of conditions for the helpee, is viewed as the key to the healing process.

EMPATHY

Helpees like to feel understood on their own terms by helpers. Empathy is the capacity to identify yourself mentally with and fully to comprehend the helpee's inner world. Helpers may possess and be perceived to show empathic understanding in relation to single helpee statements, a series of helpee statements, the whole of a helping session, or a series of helping sessions. Rogers thought helpers should possess and show an empathic attitude. He stressed creating an empathic emotional climate in the helping interview rather than using empathy as a set of skills.

Rogers' use of the term empathy particularly focused on the construct of experiencing. He attempted to improve the quantity and quality of his helpees' inner listening to the ongoing flow of psychological and physiological experiencing within them. As well as assisting helpees to get in touch with more obvious feelings, he attempted to help them sense meanings of which they were scarcely aware. However, he stopped short of trying to uncover those emotions of which helpees were totally unaware, since this might be too threatening.

Empathy is an active process in which helpers desire to know and reach out to receive helpees' communications and meanings. Responding to individual helpee statements is a process of listening and observing, resonating, discriminating, communicating and checking your understanding. Needless to say, the final and essential dimension is that the helpee has, to some extent, perceived the helper's empathy. Box 5.1, taken from a demonstration film with Rogers as the counsellor, illustrates this process. The client, Gloria, is talking about how her father could never show he cared for her the way she would have liked.

BOX 5.1 DIMENSIONS OF THE EMPATHY PROCESS

HELPEE'S STATEMENT

'I don't know what it is. You know when I talk about it it feels more flip. If I just sit still a minute, it feels like a great big hurt down there. Instead, I feel cheated.'

COUNSELLOR'S RESPONDING PROCESSES

Observing and listening: Observes and listens to the helpee's verbal, vocal and bodily communication.

Resonating: Feels some of the emotion the helpee experiences.

Discriminating: Discriminates what is really important to the helpee and formulates this into a response.

Communicating: 'It's much easier to be a little flip because then you don't feel that big lump inside of hurt.' Communicates a response that attempts to

(Continued)

(Continued)

show understanding of the helpee's thoughts, feelings and personal meanings. Accompanies verbal communication with good vocal and bodily communication.

Checking: In this instance, the helpee quickly made her next statement that followed the train of her experiencing and thought. However, the counsellor could either have waited and allowed the helpee space to respond or could have enquired if the response was accurate.

HELPEE PERCEPTION OF COUNSELLOR'S RESPONDING

How the helpee reacted indicated that she perceived the counsellor to be showing excellent empathy and that she was able to continue getting more in touch with her experiencing.

UNCONDITIONAL POSITIVE REGARD

Unconditional positive regard consists of two dimensions: level of regard and unconditionality of regard. Level of regard, or possibly more correctly level of positive regard, consists of positive helper feelings towards the helpee, such as liking, caring and warmth. Unconditionality of regard consists of a non-judgmental acceptance of the helpee's experiencing and disclosures as their subjective reality. A key issue in unconditional positive regard is that helpers are not trying to possess or control helpees to meet their own needs. Instead, helpers respect helpees' separateness and accept their unique differences. Such acceptance gives helpees permission to acknowledge and fully experience their thoughts and feelings.

Another way of looking at unconditional positive regard is that helpers respect and value the deeper core of helpees and identify with their potential – rather than with their current – behaviours. Unconditional positive regard involves compassion for human frailty and an understanding of universal conditions that lead individuals to become less effective persons than desirable. Helpees are more likely to blossom and change if prized for their human potential rather than rejected for their human failings. Though this may be setting high standards, often the inability of some helpers to feel and show unconditional positive regard reflects insufficient personal development.

CONGRUENCE

Congruence or genuineness has both an internal and an external dimension. Internally, helpers are accurately able to acknowledge significant thoughts, feelings and experiences and possess a high degree of self-awareness. This self-awareness may include acknowledging characteristics not ideal for helping: for example, 'I am afraid of this client' or 'My attention is so focused on my own problems that I am scarcely able to listen to him/her.'

Externally, helpers communicate to helpees as real persons. What helpers say and how they say it rings true. They do not hide behind professional façades or wear polite social masks. Honesty and sincerity characterize congruent communication. For example, compassionate and caring helpers live these qualities in helping encounters. Their verbal, vocal and bodily communication sends consistent caring messages. They are not portraying how they think they should be but communicating how they truly are in those moments.

Congruence does not mean 'letting it all hang out'. Helpers are able to use their awareness of their own thoughts and feelings to nurture and develop their helpees. Though congruence may include personal disclosures, these disclosures should be for the benefit of helpees in the interest of humanizing the helping process and moving it forward and not in order to make helpers feel more comfortable.

SOME DEFICIENCIES IN OFFERING THE CORE CONDITIONS

A common factor in all deficiencies in offering the core conditions is that the helper's responses insufficiently reflect the helpees' emotional states and communications. For instance, helpers who keep questioning helpees fail to provide the empathic space they need to get in touch with, explore and share what they are experiencing. Helpers who respond in judgemental ways to what helpees say are providing conditional rather than unconditional positive regard. Helpers who are insufficiently congruent in acknowledging their own thoughts, feelings and actions are going to relate to helpees in insufficiently genuine or congruent ways. In brief, all these deficiencies, however openly or subtly they get transmitted, show that the helper is not accurately responding to the helpee.

COMMUNICATION PROCESSES AND PATTERNS

Helping relationships are processes of two-way communication for good or ill. For example, during helping sessions and contacts, helpers and helpees are in a continuous process of sending, receiving, evaluating and interpreting verbal, vocal and bodily communication.

One way to look at the communication processes involved in helping relationships is in terms of how helpers and helpees reward one another. For example, helper communications like active listening, warmth and invitations for clients to become involved in the process can each be rewarding to helpees. Helpees also provide rewards to their helpers, for instance, smiles and head nods.

As in any relationship, helpers and helpees can build up mutually reinforcing communication patterns, which can enhance or impede the helping process. A helpful pattern of communication is one that is collaborative in attaining legitimate helping goals. For example, good empathic responses from helpers elicit honest self-exploring responses from helpees, which in turn elicit good empathic responses from helpers, and so on. The demand–withdrawal pattern is an example of an unhelpful pattern of communication. Here, helpers continually seek personal data from helpees who constantly withdraw in the face of such attempts because they are not ready to reveal the required information. On the other hand, sometimes under-confident helpers are too reticent in seeking information. Another negative communication pattern is that between charismatic or domineering helpers and dependent helpees.

THE COLLABORATIVE RELATIONSHIP

A good way to look at successful helping relationships, especially those that extend over a period of time, is to consider whether they are collaborative. This is a valuable criterion, whether helpers are using counselling skills in quasi-counselling roles, as part of other primary roles, or as voluntary helpers, or are providing one another with peer support. The notion of collaboration implies that helpees cooperate with helpers because they feel understood by them and, within the limitations of the contexts in which they encounter one another, feel some kind of positive emotional bond with them. Collaborative relationships also assume that helpers and helpees are working towards mutual goals. Furthermore, collaboration entails helpees being comfortable with the tasks and methods employed in helping.

Activity 5.1   Offering helping relationships

1 Think of a time when someone has really helped you with a problem and/or to feel better. What characteristics or skills did your helper use?
2 To what extent and in which ways was your helper being empathic and showing unconditional positive regard and congruence? If the helping lasted longer than a very short time, to what extent did you and your helper have a collaborative relationship?
3 Hold a brief conversation with a partner in which you give her/him the opportunity to share a concern. Afterwards, discuss what skills you used and how well you used them. Then, reverse roles.

THE HELPING PROCESS

6

CHAPTER GOALS

By studying and doing the activity in this chapter you should:

- Start thinking about the helping process systematically.
- Know about a simple model for the helping process.

Helpers see helpees in a wide variety of contexts and with many different primary and secondary agendas. Furthermore, contact with helpees may be brief and intermittent rather than on a regular basis. To assume that there is a single helping process that covers all these situations is inaccurate. Nevertheless, many helpers, helper trainers and trainees find it useful to think of the use of counselling skills with helpees as constituting a helping process.

When thinking of counselling and helping, the word process has at least two main meanings. One meaning is that of movement, the fact of something happening. Such processes can take place within helpers and helpees and between them. Furthermore, helping processes can take place outside as well as inside helping relationships, and after as well as during helping relationships. Another meaning of the word process is that of progression over time, especially a progression which involves a series of stages. The two meanings of the word process overlap in that the processes within and between helpers and helpees change as helping progresses through various stages.

Helping process models are simplified step-by-step representations of different goals and activities at progressive stages of helping. They are structured frameworks for viewing the helping process. They provide ways of assisting you to think and work more systematically. Helping process models work on the assumption that the use of helping skills is cumulative, and that insufficient application of skills in the earlier stage or stages negatively influences the ability to help in later stages.

In this chapter I present a simple three-stage model of the helping process. The underlying idea is that many helpees come to see helpers with fairly specific problems. Sometimes, the problems may have a large psychological component, like learning to assertively set limits on unwanted sexual advances. On other occasions, helpees may bring problems that, on the surface at least, do not contain complex psychological components, such as needing financial, legal or retirement planning advice.

When applying helping models, a useful distinction to bear in mind is that between an overall problem (for instance coping with sexual harassment) and specific situations within an overall problem (for instance addressing a specific episode of sexual harassment, such as dealing with a work colleague who will not take 'no' for an answer). My experience as a counselling skills trainer is that it is best to start learning how to apply a helping process by working with specific situations within overall problems rather than with overall problems in their totality. However, in some kinds of helping, for instance financial or careers advice, an approach to training based on such a distinction may not be valid.

With helping models, a further issue is that of how much to focus on identifying and changing helpees' poor mind skills and communication/action skills that may not only contribute to their current problems but also place them at risk of repeating their mistakes in future. In brief helping, you may consider that there is neither sufficient opportunity nor enough helpee motivation for addressing such underlying issues, but this need not always be the case.

THE RELATING–UNDERSTANDING–CHANGING (RUC) HELPING MODEL

In this book I present a simple Relating–Understanding–Changing (RUC) helping process model (see Box 6.1). This model is especially applicable to problem situations, but can be adapted when helpers have other agendas, for instance pregnancy advice, as well. The fact that the helping model is presented in three stages may imply a degree of tidiness inappropriate to the actual practice of helping. Often the stages overlap and sometimes you may find it necessary to move backwards and forwards between stages. Flexibility can be important.

BOX 6.1   THE RELATING–UNDERSTANDING–CHANGING (RUC) HELPING MODEL

Stage 1:	**Relating**
Main task	To start establishing a collaborative relationship.
Stage 2:	**Understanding**
Main task	To clarify and enlarge both helper and helpee understanding of the problem situation.
Stage 3:	**Changing**
Main task	To assist the helpee to change so that the problem situation is addressed more effectively than in the past.

STAGE 1: THE RELATING STAGE

Here the main helper and helpee task is to start establishing a collaborative relationship. Helping relationships start at, if not before, the point when you first meet with helpees. For instance, how you handle a telephone call may decide whether a helpee wishes to set up an appointment with you. Also, you need to become calm and get your helping space ready before you open the door of your office to meet helpees. A preliminary phase of the relating stage is the introductions phase, the purpose of which can be described as meeting, greeting and seating.

How you start a session varies according to the helping context as well as according to each participant's wishes. For example, helping contexts can require basic information gathering at the start of sessions. Apart from this, the main choice in starting a session is whether first to allow helpees to tell their stories and then do some structuring regarding the nature of the helping contact, or the reverse. My preference is for letting helpees talk first and 'get their problem(s) off their chest'. Sometimes, helpees come with one clearly identified problem situation, for example how to handle anxiety concerning an important exam in a week's time. On other occasions, they may have many or more complex problems. In any event, use active listening skills to create an emotionally safe space for helpees to share their main reasons for coming. If there is more than one problem area, you can summarize and identify the different problem areas and ask helpees which one they want to address. Then, assuming the helping contact is brief, you can ask them to identify a particular situation within the problem area on which to work together.

STAGE 2: THE UNDERSTANDING STAGE

Here the main helper and helpee task is to clarify and enlarge your understanding of the chosen problem situation. Often, helpees feel at an impasse in problem situations. Getting them to describe the situation more fully in a supportive emotional climate can loosen their thinking, enlighten them and encourage them to think that they may be able to manage it better. In the context of good active listening skills, you can use questioning skills that elicit information about helpees in relation to their problem situations. Areas in which you may ask questions include helpees' thoughts, feelings and physical reactions and how they have attempted to cope in the past, including the patterns of communication they have established with significant others. Sometimes you can engage helpees in mini-role-plays that can go some way to eliciting the actual verbal, vocal and bodily communications that they have employed in the problem situations.

Helpers seek to enlarge as well as to clarify the helpees' understanding of such situations, including their contribution to sustaining negative aspects of them. You may ask questions that elicit information relevant to the helpees' mental processes, for instance about their self-talk, rules and perceptions. Sometimes you may challenge helpee perceptions and provide feedback. Furthermore, at appropriate junctures, you may summarize the ground recently covered. In addition, at the end of the understanding stage, you can summarize all the main points elicited so far and check with helpees about the accuracy of your summary and whether they wish to modify, add or subtract anything.

STAGE 3: THE CHANGING STAGE

Here, the main helper and helpee task is for helpees to change so that they deal with problem situations more effectively than in the past. Helpers and helpees set goals and develop and implement strategies to address problem situations and to communicate, act and think better. Furthermore, you attend to how helpees can maintain helpful changes.

Two somewhat overlapping approaches that helpers and helpees can take to the changing stage are the facilitating problem-solving approach and the improving communications/actions and mind skills approach. In the facilitating problem-solving approach, you assist helpees to clarify goals for problem situations, generate and explore options to attain them, and develop and implement action plans.

In the improving communications/actions and mind skills approach, you and your helpees work together to specify communication and mind skills goals and the strategies to attain each of them. You may explore options in regard of which goals to set. Often, statements of goals can include not only what helpees want to achieve but the communication they want to avoid as well. You can assist helpees to develop plans to attain their communication and mind skills goals. Frequently, you act as a client-centred or helpee-centred coach in assisting helpees to develop more effective verbal, vocal and body messages for their problem situations. Avoid controlling helpees, assuming responsibility for their problems, and making their decisions for them. Instead, encourage autonomy by ensuring that they 'own' their problems. Skilled helpers draw out helpees' ideas and give them confidence in their own resources for handling their problem situations.

Sometimes coaching includes role-playing. Some helpers incorporate the use of the whiteboard into coaching: for instance, jointly formulating with a helpee a clear verbal request for someone to change their behaviour and then pinpointing desirable vocal and body messages to back up this request. In addition, you can encourage helpees to think more effectively. For instance, once helpees have identified useful ways of communicating in their problem situations, you can coach them in helpful self-talk for rehearsing and enacting this behaviour in real life. Furthermore, you can assist helpees to challenge unrealistic rules and perceptions and replace them with more realistic ones.

Encourage helpees to rehearse and practise their new skills of thinking and communicating between sessions, and then have them report back at the start of subsequent sessions. Assist them to assume responsibility for changing their behaviour both now and in the future. Before helping concludes, you and the helpee can review ways in which they can maintain beneficial changes made.

BOX 6.2   CASE EXAMPLES

EXAMPLE 1: HELPING A SHY PUPIL TO MAKE FRIENDS

Rick, 16, discusses her problem of shyness with Mohammed, 37, a secondary-school teacher with counselling skills. Mohammed first builds a relationship with Rick by sensitively allowing him to share his thoughts and feelings about his difficulties. He then gently probes how Rick behaves in specific situations where he wants to meet people, asking him about what he thinks as well as about what, if anything, he says and how he says it. Rick and Mohammed then draw up a simple plan in which he is to make initial contact with two pupils at school with whom he wants to be friends. They focus on where he will contact them and on how to do so. They also discuss what he will do if successful and also if unsuccessful.

EXAMPLE 2: HELPING THE WIFE OF A HUSBAND SUFFERING FROM DEMENTIA

Lily, 59, who helps out at a counselling service for older people, sees Kate, 78, who is finding living with her husband Joshua, 84, increasingly difficult as his dementia gets worse. Lily first builds a relationship by giving Kate the opportunity and space to talk about her life. She then gently broadens Kate's perspective by asking some questions not only about how she copes with Joshua, but also about how she looks after herself. Together they then discuss ways in which Kate can get some support that allows her time for herself. They also discuss ways in which Kate can think differently about her life and not keep thinking of herself only as an extension of Joshua's dementia.

EXAMPLE 3: HELPING A WORKER TO BECOME MORE ASSERTIVE

Amelia, 36, a supervisor in a clothing store, hires new worker, Kusum, 20, as a salesperson. Noticing that Kusum holds back from engaging with customers, Amelia takes her aside and builds a relationship with Kusum within which she explains how she feels starting the job and her difficulties going up to customers,

(Continued)

(Continued)

answering their questions and telling them about clothes in which they might be interested. Amelia encourages Kusum to describe in some detail how she behaves verbally, vocally and bodily when she sees a customer and also what is going through her mind. Amelia and Kusum then discuss how she might think and behave differently. They agree on some simple assertiveness skills, such as using some key verbal, vocal and body messages for confidently asking customers if they need help and then directly answering their questions. Amelia and Kusum role-play using these skills effectively, with Amelia playing the customer.

Activity 6.1   Exploring the helping process

1   Do you think it useful to think of the helping process in three stages?
2   Think of a problem situation in your own life that you would like to improve. However, if you are on your own you cannot do the relating stage, so instead use the understanding stage and the changing stage in relation to it.
3   For each of the examples in Box 6.2, using the Relating–Understanding–Changing model, how might you assist the helpee to understand their problem(s) and to explore change?

II

SPECIFIC COUNSELLING SKILLS

UNDERSTANDING THE INTERNAL FRAME OF REFERENCE

CHAPTER GOALS

By studying and doing the activities in this chapter you should:

- Know what active listening is.
- Know the difference between the external and the internal frame of reference.

How many people do you know who listen to you properly? Most of us know relatively few. Quite apart from wanting airtime to speak about their own thoughts, feelings and experiences, many people we know will put their own 'spin' on what we say rather than listen accurately and deeply to us. The single most important goal of any basic counselling and helping skills course is to improve the quality of trainees' listening. Even experienced counsellors and helpers have to monitor the quality of their listening all the time.

USE ACTIVE LISTENING

Two counsellors meet in a lift at the end of a working day. One is looking fresh, the other tired.

Tired-looking counsellor: I don't know how you can look so fresh after all that listening.

Fresh-looking counsellor: Who listens?

How can you create an emotional climate so that helpees feel safe and free to talk with you? Many of the component skills of creating collaborative relationships come under the heading of active listening. A distinction exists between hearing and listening. *Hearing* involves the capacity to be aware of and to receive sounds. *Listening* involves not only receiving sounds but, as much as possible, accurately understanding their meaning. As such it entails hearing and memorizing words, being sensitive to vocal cues, observing body language, and taking into account the personal and social context of communications. However, you can listen accurately without being a rewarding listener. *Active listening* entails not only accurately understanding speakers' communications, but also showing that you have understood. As such, active listening involves being skilled in both receiving and sending communications.

Active listening is the fundamental skill of any helping relationship. Nevertheless, throughout the Relating–Understanding–Changing (RUC) helping model, you should adapt how you use active listening in the different stages of the model. Furthermore, if the model is unsuitable for the kind of helping contacts you have, you can adapt your skills of active listening accordingly. However, if you are unable to listen properly in the first place, you are poorly equipped to integrate active listening with other counselling skills, such as the ability to ask questions in an appropriate manner.

POSSESS AN ATTITUDE OF RESPECT AND ACCEPTANCE

Four kinds of listening take place in any person-to-person helping conversation. Listening takes place between helper and helpee and within each party. The quality of your inner listening, or being appropriately sensitive to your own thoughts and feelings, may be vital to the quality of your outer listening. If either you or the helpee listens either poorly or excessively to yourself, you listen less well to one another. Conversely, if either or both listen well to one another, this may help the quality of your inner listening.

An accepting attitude involves respecting helpees as separate human beings with rights to their own thoughts and feelings. Such an attitude entails suspending judgement on helpees' perceived goodness or badness. All humans are fallible and possess good and poor human skills or capabilities that may result in either happiness or suffering for themselves and others. Respect comes from the Latin word *respicere*, meaning to look at. Respect means the ability to look at others as they are and to prize their unique individuality. Respect also means allowing other people to grow and develop on their own terms without exploitation and control. Though an accepting attitude involves respecting others as separate and unique human beings, this does not mean that you need to agree with everything helpees say. Ideally, however, you are secure enough in yourself to respect what they say as being their versions of reality.

You need to be psychologically present to helpees. This entails the absence of defensiveness and a willingness to allow helpees' expressions and experiencing to affect you. As much as possible, helpers should be 'all there' – with your body, thoughts, senses and emotions. Psychological accessibility entails an accepting attitude not only to helpees, but also to yourself. Put simply, a confident person's acceptance of self translates into acceptance of others, and the reverse is also true.

UNDERSTAND THE HELPEE'S INTERNAL FRAME OF REFERENCE

Taking the helpee's perspective and seeing things how they see them are other ways of describing the ability to understand helpees from their internal frame of reference. There is an American Indian proverb that states: 'Don't judge any person until you have walked two moons in their moccasins.' If helpees are to feel that you receive them loud and clear, you need to develop the ability to 'walk in their moccasins', 'get inside their skins' and 'see the world through their eyes'. At the heart of active listening is a basic distinction between 'you' and 'me', between 'your view of you' and 'my view of you', and between 'your view of me' and 'my view of me'. Your view of you and my view of me are inside or internal perspectives, whereas your view of me and my view of you are outside or external perspectives.

The skill of listening to and understanding helpees is based on choosing to acknowledge the separateness between 'me' and 'you' by getting inside their internal frame of reference rather than remaining in your own external frame of reference. If you respond to what helpees say in ways that show accurate understanding of their perspectives, you respond as if inside the helpees' internal frame of reference. However, if you choose not to show understanding of your helpees' perspectives or lack the skills to understand them, you respond from the external frame of reference. Box 7.1 provides examples of helper responses from external and internal frames of reference.

BOX 7.1   HELPER RESPONSES FROM INTERNAL AND EXTERNAL FRAMES OF REFERENCE

EXTERNAL FRAME OF REFERENCE RESPONSES

You shouldn't have spoken to her that way.

Well, I wouldn't have done that.

You let yourself get upset far too easily.

You could have acted differently.

INTERNAL FRAME OF REFERENCE RESPONSES

You're glad that she has come home.

You feel annoyed when he keeps repeating himself.

You have mixed feelings about your promotion. Pleased at the extra money and status, yet frightened about the extra responsibility.

You're worried about seeing her again.

Often you can show that you are taking your helpees' internal frame of reference by starting your response with 'You'. However, as the statements 'You shouldn't have spoken to her that way' and 'You could have acted differently' indicate, helpers can make responses starting with the word 'You' from the external frame of reference too.

You should always consciously choose whether or not to respond as if inside your helpees' internal frame of reference. Think of a three-link chain: helpee statement–helper response–helpee statement. Helpers who respond from helpees' internal frames of reference allow them to choose either to continue on the same path or to change direction. However, if helpers respond from their external frames of reference, they can influence helpees in such a way as to divert or block those trains of thoughts, feelings and experiences that they might otherwise have chosen.

Activity 7.1   Identifying the helpee's internal frame of reference

Below are some statement–response excerpts from formal and informal helping situations. Three helper responses have been provided for each statement. Write 'IN' or 'EX' by each response according to whether it reflects the helpee's internal perspective or comes from the helper's external perspective. Some of the responses may seem artificial, but they have been chosen to highlight the point of the exercise. Answers are provided at the end of this chapter.

For example:

PATIENT TO NURSE

Patient: I'm having difficulty moving around after my operation.

Nurse:

EX (a) Can't you try a bit harder?

IN (b) You're finding it hard to get about.

EX (c) Take that up with your doctor.

1: EMPLOYEE TO MANAGER

Employee: I would like to know how I am doing and ways in which I might improve.

Manager:

_____ (a) Can't you answer those questions for yourself?

_____ (b) You will have to wait until your annual evaluation.

_____ (c) You want some feedback on how you are getting on and might do better.

2: HELPEE TO RELATIONSHIP COUNSELLOR

Client: I'm fed up with him/her not doing their share of the housework.

Social worker:

_____ (a) You're exasperated with him/her not pulling his/her weight.
_____ (b) Well, a lot of people are in the same boat.
_____ (c) I would be fed up too if I were in your shoes.

3: CLIENT TO HELPER

Client: I'm unhappy because there is nobody I'm close to here.

Helper:

_____ (a) Many people take time to adjust to a new location and make friends.
_____ (b) You're lonely because you've no real friends here.
_____ (c) Well, you should stop feeling so sorry for yourself and look for friends harder.

Activity 7.2   Observing and assessing internal and external responses

1   Watch and listen to television and radio interviews and chat shows. Observe the extent to which interviewers respond from the interviewee's internal frame of reference.
2   Monitor your own communication for a week and become more aware of when you respond to speakers from your own or from their frame of reference:

- in helping contacts
- in daily life.

Answers to Activity 7.1

(a) EX   (b) EX   (c) IN
(a) IN   (b) EX   (c) EX
(a) EX   (b) IN   (c) EX

SHOWING ATTENTION AND INTEREST

CHAPTER GOALS

By studying and doing the activities in this chapter you should:

- Become more aware of good and less-good body messages a helper can send.
- Start assessing how good your body messages are.
- Improve your ability to show attention and interest to helpees.

When together, helpers and helpees always send messages to one another. In Chapter 2, I mentioned that there were five main ways of sending communication/action skills messages: namely, verbal, vocal, bodily, touch and taking action messages. This chapter aims to build your skills of sending good body messages to helpees. Your body messages as listeners are important both when listening and responding to them. To be a rewarding person with whom to talk, you need physically to convey your emotional availability and interest. Often this is referred to as attending behaviour.

Body messages are the main category of helper responses when helpees are speaking. A simple example of what not to do may highlight the point. Imagine being a helpee who comes to a helper for assistance with a sensitive personal problem and, when the helper asks you to say why you have come, she or he looks out of the window and puts their feet up on the desk. On a more serious note, when a counselling graduate student at Stanford University, I had an excellent client-centred counsellor who was the Director of what was then called the Counseling and Testing Center. Every now and then he would put his feet up on his desk in a relaxed manner. However, by then, I knew he was still attending closely to me and I did not find his behaviour off-putting.

The following suggestions include some of the main body message skills that demonstrate interest and attention. In varying degrees, they provide non-verbal rewards for talking. I offer this list of suggestions with the proviso that those who see helpees in non-office settings will have to edit or adapt the suggestions to your different helping contexts.

BE AVAILABLE

It may seem obvious, but helpers may sometimes rightly or wrongly be perceived as insufficiently available to help. You may be overworked. You may be poor at letting your availability or any limits on it be known. Intentionally or unintentionally you may send messages that create distance. For instance, a minority of college and university lecturers may rarely be around in their office hours for discussing students' concerns. In addition, they may spend as little time on campus as they can get away with. Send clear messages to helpees and others about availability and access. One simple way to indicate availability in informal helping settings is just to go over and be near or chat to people.

ADOPT A RELAXED AND OPEN BODY POSTURE

A relaxed body posture, without slumping or slouching, contributes to the message that a helper is receptive. If you sit in a tense and uptight fashion, helpees may consciously or intuitively feel that you are too bound up in your personal agendas and unfinished business to be fully accessible.

Helpers and helpees need to sit with an open body posture so that you can easily see one another. Some counselling skills trainers recommend sitting square to clients – the helper's left shoulder opposite the helpee's right shoulder. However, another option is to sit at a slight angle to helpees. Here, both of you can still receive all of one another's significant facial and bodily messages. The advantage of this is that it provides each of you with more discretion in varying the directness of your contact than if sitting opposite one another. Highly vulnerable helpees may especially appreciate this seating arrangement.

How you use your arms and legs can enhance or detract from an open body posture. For example, crossed arms can be perceived as barriers – sometimes, crossed legs can too. There is some research evidence that suggests that postural similarity, where two people take up mirror-image postures, is perceived as a sign of liking.

AVOID LEANING TOO FAR FORWARDS OR BACKWARDS

Whether you lean forwards, backwards or sideways is another aspect of your body posture. If you lean too far forwards you look odd, and helpees may experience an invasion of their personal space. However, in moments of intimate disclosure, a marked forwards lean may build rapport rather than be perceived as intrusive. If you lean too far back, helpees may find this posture to be distancing.

USE APPROPRIATE GAZE AND EYE CONTACT

Gaze means looking at people in the area of their faces. Good gaze skills indicate your interest and enable you to receive important facial messages. Gaze can give you cues about when to stop listening and start responding. However, the main cues used in synchronizing conversation are verbal and voice messages rather than body messages.

Good eye contact skills involve looking in helpees' direction in order to allow the possibility of your eyes meeting reasonably often. There is an equilibrium level for eye contact in any helping relationship depending on the degree of anxiety in helpee and helper, how developed the relationship is, and the degree of attraction involved. Staring can threaten helpees because they may feel dominated or seen through. I once had a helpee who started counselling by sitting with one hand shielding his eyes, looking 90 degrees from me, and only occasionally taking a quick peek in my direction. It took about eight sessions for him gradually to move towards a normal amount of eye contact. Helpees want an appropriate amount of eye contact from helpers and may perceive you as tense or bored if you look down or away too often.

CONVEY APPROPRIATE FACIAL EXPRESSIONS

When discussing feelings in Chapter 2, I mentioned the seven important feelings – happiness, interest, surprise, fear, sadness, anger, and disgust or contempt – each of which can be conveyed by facial expressions. People's faces are their main way of sending body messages about feelings. Much facial information is conveyed through the mouth and eyebrows. A friendly, relaxed facial expression, including a smile, usually demonstrates interest. However, as the helpee talks, your facial expressions need to show that you are tuned into what they say. For instance, if helpees are happy, serious, weeping or angry, you need to adjust your facial expression to indicate that you understand their feelings.

USE GOOD GESTURES

Gestures are body movements used to convey thoughts and feelings. Perhaps the head nod is the most common gesture in listening, with small ones to show continued attention, larger and repeated ones to indicate agreement. Head nods can be viewed as rewards to helpees to continue talking. On the negative side, selective head nods can also be powerful ways of controlling helpees. Then unconditional acceptance becomes conditional acceptance.

Gestures may also illustrate shapes, sizes or movements, particularly when these are difficult to describe in words. You can respond with arm and hand gestures to show attention and interest. However, using expressive arm gestures too much or too little can be off-putting. Negative gestures that can display inattentiveness and discourage helpees from clear communication include fidgeting with pens and pencils, hands clenched together, finger drumming, fiddling with your hair, putting a hand over your mouth, ear tugging, and scratching yourself, among others.

USE TOUCH SPARINGLY

Touching helpees may be appropriate in helping, though great care needs to be taken that it is not an unwanted invasion of personal space. For example, demonstrations of concern may include touching a helpee's hands, arms, shoulders and upper back. The intensity and duration of touch should be sufficient to establish contact yet avoid discomfort and any hint of sexual interest. Part of being an active listener includes picking up messages about the limits and desirability of your use of touch. As porcupine parents advise their offspring about making love, when contemplating touching clients, 'proceed with caution'.

BE SENSITIVE TO PERSONAL SPACE AND HEIGHT

Active listening entails respecting helpees' personal space. You can be too close or too far away. Perhaps a comfortable physical distance for helpers and helpees is sitting with your heads about five feet apart. In Western cultures helpees might perceive any shorter distance as too personal. If you are physically too far away, not only do helpees have to talk louder, but they may perceive you as emotionally distant. The most comfortable height for helping conversations is with both of your heads at the same level. Those helpers sitting in higher and more elaborate chairs than helpees can contribute to the latter feeling less powerful in the relationship.

BE CAREFUL ABOUT CLOTHING AND GROOMING

Sometimes, helpers' clothes are governed by the contexts in which they work; for instance in hospitals doctors wear white coats and nurses wear uniforms. On many other occasions you can choose how you dress. Your clothes send messages about you that can influence how much and in which areas helpees reveal themselves. These messages include social and occupational standing, sex-role identity, ethnicity, degree of conformity to peer group norms, rebelliousness and how outgoing or introverted you are. While maintaining individuality, you need to dress appropriately for your clientele; for example, delinquent teenagers respond better to informally dressed helpers than do stressed business executives. Your personal grooming also provides important information about how well you take care of yourself, for instance, clean or dirty, neat or untidy. In addition, the length and styling of your hair sends messages about you.

CONCLUDING COMMENTS

The concept of rules is very important for understanding the appropriateness of body messages. However, rules governing behaviour in helping situations should not be straitjackets and, sometimes, you may need to bend or break the rules to create genuinely collaborative helping relationships. Relationship rules also differ across cultures. For instance, to some Australian Aboriginal people it is unacceptable to look others straight in the eye. Another example is that in India it is not uncommon for people either to nod *or* shake or to nod *and* shake their heads to mean yes or no. In short, you require sensitivity to the body message rules of the social and cultural contexts in which you work as well as to your own and helpees' individual needs.

You require flexibility in making active listening choices that entail bodily communication. As helping relationships develop, helpees get to know whether and when you are receptive to them. For instance, helpees may know from past experience that when you lean back you are still very attentive. Use body messages showing attention and interest selectively. If necessary, you can choose to make your body messages less rewarding: for instance, when you want to check your understanding of what helpees say, stop them from rambling on, or make points of your own.

Genuineness is important. Both within your body messages and also between your body messages and your voice and verbal messages, consistency increases the chances of helpees perceiving you as a rewarding listener. On the other hand, you may smile, yet at the same time either fidget or foot tap. The smile may indicate interest, the fidgeting and foot tapping impatience, and the overall message conveys insincerity. In addition, you may make good verbal responses that can be completely negated by poor bodily communication.

Activity 8.1 Raising awareness of good and poor body messages

Your partner talks about a topic of interest to her/him and your role is mainly to listen; however:

- start for a minute or so by using terrible body messages when you respond, then
- switch for two or more minutes to using good body messages
- then hold a debriefing period in which you discuss what it felt like sending and receiving terrible and good body messages
- reverse roles and repeat the steps above.

Activity 8.2 Assessing body messages for showing attention and interest

To the extent that they are relevant to the helping setting(s) in which you either use or will use counselling skills, assess yourself on each of the following body messages for showing attention and interest:

- being available
- adopting a relaxed and open body posture
- avoiding leaning too far forwards or backwards
- using appropriate gaze
- using appropriate eye contact
- conveying appropriate facial expressions
- using good gestures
- using touch sparingly
- being sensitive to personal space and height
- being careful about clothing and grooming
- cultural considerations in how you communicate with your body
- other important areas not listed above.

Activity 8.3 Improving showing attention and interest

Pick a specific body message for showing attention and interest that you think you might improve: for instance, you may have a tendency to sit with too rigid a posture. Then hold a conversation with a partner where you work on improving your chosen body message. Either during or at the end of your conversation ask for feedback on how you are doing. Afterwards, if appropriate, reverse roles with your partner.

PARAPHRASING AND REFLECTING FEELINGS

9

CHAPTER GOALS

By studying and doing the activities in this chapter you should:

- Be introduced to paraphrasing and reflecting feelings skills.
- Know about offering small verbal rewards and open-ended questions.

The next two somewhat overlapping skills, paraphrasing and reflecting feelings, involve helpers feeding back to helpees what they have just communicated. You may wonder 'Why bother?' or think 'Isn't this all rather artificial?' Your verbalizations of helpee statements provide rewards for them to continue. Furthermore, helpees' experiences may seem more real to them if they verbalize rather than just think them, and even more real when they then hear these experiences verbalized again by you. Such verbalizations may put them more in touch with their own thoughts, feelings and experiences. In addition, by verbalizing what helpees communicate, you and the helpee can engage in a process of exploring and understanding more accurately the meaning of what they communicate.

PARAPHRASING SKILLS

A paraphrase expresses the meaning of a helpee statement or series of statements in different words. On some occasions, you may choose to repeat rather than paraphrase helpees' words. For instance, if a helpee shares a significant insight, it may help the insight sink in if you repeat the helpee's words. However, more often than not, repetition becomes parroting. Helpees want to relate to persons, not parrots!

Paraphrasing involves rewording at least the crux of the helpee's message. You try to convey back to them clearly and briefly what they have just communicated from their internal frame of reference. When you paraphrase, you may sometimes use their words, but sparingly. They try to stay close to the kind of language that each helpee uses. Box 9.1 provides examples of paraphrasing.

BOX 9.1   EXAMPLES OF PARAPHRASING

HELPEE TO SOCIAL WORKER

Helpee: I keep trying not to mind about it, but I still do.

Social worker: You make a real effort not to care about it, but you keep doing so.

PUPIL TO TEACHER

Pupil: I'm very glad to be studying with you.

Teacher: You're delighted to be learning with me.

A good paraphrase can provide mirror reflections that are clearer and sometimes more succinct than original statements. If so, helpees may show appreciation with comments like: 'That's right' or 'You've got me'. A simple tip for those of you who struggle with paraphrasing is to slow the helping conversation down, thus providing more time to think. Another tip for gaining confidence and fluency is to practise paraphrasing both in and out of class.

REFLECTING FEELINGS SKILLS

Most helper responses that reflect feelings are paraphrases that emphasize the emotional content of helpees' communications. Reflecting or mirroring feelings is the main skill of active listening. In Chapter 5, I described a five-stage empathy process: observing and listening, resonating, discriminating, communicating and checking. Here I collapse this process into the two stages of identifying feelings and reflecting feelings.

IDENTIFYING FEELINGS

Before you can reflect a helpee's feelings back to them, you need accurately to identify or discriminate what they are. Sometimes helpees say 'I feel' when they mean 'I think'. For example, 'I feel that equality between the sexes is essential' describes a thought rather than a feeling. On the other hand, 'I feel angry about sex discrimination' describes a feeling. It is important that you distinguish between helpees' thoughts and feelings, if you wish to be skilful at picking up feelings accurately. What follows are ways of identifying feelings.

- *Body messages*   You can pick up much about what your helpee feels from just looking at them. For example, helpees may come for help looking tired, worried or happy. They may slump in the chair or sit upright. Sometimes helpees send mixed messages in which their body messages are more important than their verbal messages.
- *Vocal messages*   Many of the messages about the intensity of helpees' feelings are conveyed by the degree of vocal emphasis they place on them. For example, helpees very out of touch with their capacity to feel may communicate in rather flat and distant voices.
- *Feelings words and phrases*   A good but not infallible way to discover what a helpee feels is to listen to their feelings words and phrases. Feelings words include happy, sad, angry, lonely, anxious and depressed. Feelings phrases are groupings of words that describe feelings. Listening to feelings words may seem a simple guideline, but sometimes you may not listen carefully enough and then ask clients 'What did you feel?' after helpees have just said this.
- *Physical reactions words*   You can also identify feelings by listening to helpees' physical reactions words. They may describe physical reactions with words like tense, tired, pounding heart and headache.
- *Feelings idioms*   Feelings idioms are everyday expressions or turns of phrase used to communicate feelings. Very often such idioms are expressed in visual images, for example, 'I'm over the moon' is a feelings idiom describing the emotion of joy.
- *Feelings imagery*   Helpees can intentionally use visual images to conjure up and communicate feelings. The visual image provides a frame for understanding the feelings content of their messages. For instance, to describe and illustrate embarrassment, helpees might use the images of 'I felt like crawling into a corner' or 'I felt like running out of the room'.

REFLECTING FEELINGS

A simple guideline for reflecting feelings is to start responses with the personal pronoun 'you' to indicate being, 'as if' inside a helpee's internal frames of reference. When reflecting feelings it is cumbersome always to put 'You feel' before feelings words and phrases. Sometimes 'You're' is sufficient, for example, 'You're delighted' instead of 'You feel delighted'. Even better is to paraphrase and find different words to describe helpees' feelings.

Whenever possible try to communicate back a helpee's *main feeling*. Even though helpees may not start with their main feeling, they may feel better understood if you reflect their main feeling at the front of your response.

Try to reflect the *strength of feelings*. For instance, after a row, the helpee may feel 'devastated' (strong feeling), 'upset' (moderate feeling), or 'slightly upset' (weak feeling). Sometimes helpees use many words to describe their feelings. The words may cluster around the same theme, in which case you may choose to reflect the crux of the feeling. Alternatively, helpees may verbalize varying degrees of *mixed feelings* ranging from simple opposites, for instance 'happy/sad' to more complex combinations, such as 'hurt/ anger/guilt'. Good reflections pick up all key elements of feelings messages. On occasion you can assist helpees to find the right way to express their feelings. Here, reflecting feelings involves assisting them to choose *feelings words that resonate*.

Sometimes you can reflect helpees' *feelings and reasons* that they offer for them. A simple way of doing this is to make a 'You feel … because …' statement that mirrors their internal frame of reference. Reflecting back reasons does not mean that you make an interpretation or offer an explanation from your own perspective.

It is crucial that you *check the accuracy* of your reflections of feelings. You can respond to feelings statements with differing degrees of tentativeness depending on how clearly the feelings were communicated and how confident you feel about receiving these messages accurately. Almost invariably check by using slightly raised voice inflections towards the end of your responses. On other occasions, you can check by asking directly, for instance, 'Do I understand you properly?' Alternatively, you may make comments like 'I think I hear you saying (state feelings tentatively) …' or 'I want to understand what you're feeling, but I'm still not altogether clear'. Another option is to reflect back a mixed message, for instance, 'On the one hand you are saying you don't mind. On the other hand, you seem tearful.' After a pause you might add: 'I'm wondering if you are putting on a brave face?'

An important consideration in reflecting feelings is to understand whether and to what extent helpees possess insight into themselves, for example, acknowledging shame, anger, hurt or betrayal. You need to be sensitive about how much reality they can handle at any given moment in the helping process. You can threaten helpees by prematurely or clumsily reflecting feelings that they experience difficulty in acknowledging.

Box 9.2 provides examples of different ways in which helpers can reflect helpees' feelings. I do not mean to imply that there is a single correct way of responding to any of the helpee statements. Reflections of feelings, such as those offered below, can be stepping stones or bridges to helpees for further experiencing, expressing, exploring and understanding their feelings. Feelings, like ocean waves, are in a constant process of movement. Skilled helpers are able to follow and reflect the ebb and flow of helpees' feelings.

BOX 9.2   EXAMPLES OF REFLECTING FEELINGS

REFLECTING FEELINGS WORDS

Helpee: I'm afraid.

Helper: You're frightened.

(Continued)

(Continued)

REFLECTING FEELINGS PHRASES

Helpee: I feel down in the dumps.

Helper: You feel depressed.

REFLECTING PHYSICAL REACTIONS

Here, if the physical reaction is literally named, there is a case for repetition to show that you have clearly registered it. Otherwise, consider paraphrasing.

Helpee A: I start sweating.

Helper A: You begin sweating.

Helpee B: I experience butterflies in my stomach.

Helper B: You feel tension in your stomach.

REFLECTING FEELINGS AND REASONS

Helpee: I'm exhausted with attempting to complete all things.

Helper: You're really tired because you're trying to finish everything.

SMALL VERBAL REWARDS

When assisting helpees to share their internal frames of reference, you do not have to reflect every statement that they make. In addition to using good body message skills, you can use small verbal rewards. Small verbal rewards are brief expressions of helper interest designed to encourage helpees to continue talking. The message they convey is 'I am with you. Please go on.' You can use small verbal rewards for good or ill. On the one hand, they can reward helpees for sharing and exploring their internal frames of reference. On the other hand, use of small verbal rewards may subtly or crudely attempt to shape what helpees say. For instance, you may reward helpees for saying either positive or negative things about themselves. Furthermore, you can selectively reward helpees for talking about agendas of personal interest to you. Box 9.3 provides some examples of small verbal rewards, though perhaps the most frequently used, 'Uh-hum', is more vocal than verbal.

BOX 9.3   EXAMPLES OF SMALL VERBAL REWARDS

Uh-hum	Sure
Please continue	Indeed
Tell me more	And …
Go on	So …
I see	Really?
Oh?	Right
Then …	Yes
I hear you	

OPEN-ENDED QUESTIONS

In addition to reflecting feelings and small verbal rewards, you may use open-ended questions in ways that help helpees to elaborate their internal frames of reference. Such questions allow them to share their internal viewpoints without curtailing their options. A good use of open-ended questions is when, in the initial session, you wish to assist helpees to say why they have come. In subsequent sessions, too, you are likely to find open-ended questions useful. Open-ended questions include: 'Tell me about it?', 'Please elaborate?' and, slightly less open-ended, 'How do you feel about that?'

Open-ended questions may be contrasted with closed questions that curtail speakers' options: indeed they often give only two options, 'yes' or 'no'. I am not suggesting that you never use closed questions. It depends on the goals of your listening. Furthermore, many of you have to ask closed questions to perform other primary roles. Closed questions can be essential for collecting information. However, show restraint when you wish to help others share their worlds on their own terms.

Open-ended question: How was that for you?

Closed questions: Was your day good or bad?
Did that upset you?

Activity 9.1   Paraphrasing skills

1 Go back to Box 9.1 and provide at least one alternative paraphrase to each of the two helpee statements.
2 Working in a pair, each partner 'feeds' one another statements. Listeners paraphrase speakers' statements and speakers provide feedback on their reactions to each paraphrase. One option is for partners to alternate roles after each statement–response–feedback unit.

Activity 9.2   Reflecting feelings skills

1 Reproduce Box 9.2, providing your own examples of helpers reflecting their helpees' feelings in each of these areas:

- reflecting feelings words
- reflecting feelings phrases
- reflecting physical reactions
- reflecting feelings and reasons.

2 Work with a partner. Each person takes turns to be speaker and listener. The speaker picks a topic about which s/he feels comfortable sharing their feelings. When listening, help the speaker to talk about her/his feelings by reflecting them accurately. When both listening and responding pay attention to vocal and body messages as well as to verbal ones.

STARTING, STRUCTURING AND SUMMARIZING

CHAPTER GOALS

By studying and doing the activity in this chapter you should:

- Know some ways of giving helpees permission to talk.
- Learn about making statements that structure your time together.
- Know some ways of summarizing what helpees have communicated.

Good beginnings increase the chances of good middles and good endings. Poor beginnings can either lose helpees or lose ground in helping that may then be hard to retrieve. Whether in formal or informal settings, you can start the helping process in friendly and functional ways. The appropriate way to start helping varies according to the different roles that helpers play. Those of you using counselling skills as part of other roles or in informal settings will need to adjust to your own circumstances some of the skills suggested here.

PERMISSIONS TO TALK

Permissions to talk are brief statements inviting helpees to tell their stories and indicating that you are prepared to listen. Permissions to talk are 'door openers' that give the message 'I'm interested and prepared to listen. Please share with me your internal frame of reference.' You are there to discover information about them and to assist them to discover information about themselves.

You should be careful about using common opening remarks like 'How can I help you?' or 'What can I do for you?' Such remarks can get initial sessions off to unfortunate starts by suggesting that helpees are dependent on your resources rather than on developing their own resources for later self-help.

When giving helpees permission to talk, your body and vocal messages are very important in indicating that you are a comfortable and trustworthy person with whom to talk. Speaking clearly and relatively slowly may help to create a calm environment. You should also use appropriate body messages for showing attention and interest, an area already reviewed in Chapter 8.

Many of you have informal contacts with helpees outside of formal helping sessions, for instance correctional officers in facilities for delinquents, residential staff in halfway houses for former drug addicts, or nurses in hospitals. Here you may use permissions to talk, for instance when you sense that someone has a worrisome personal agenda, but requires that extra bit of encouragement to share it. Box 10.1 provides some suggestions for permissions to talk for use in both formal and informal helping. In addition, I include some follow-up statements that you can use when you become aware that helpees are having difficulty getting started.

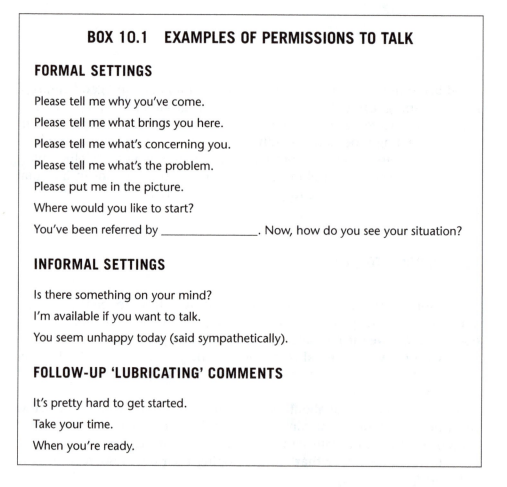

BOX 10.1   EXAMPLES OF PERMISSIONS TO TALK

FORMAL SETTINGS

Please tell me why you've come.

Please tell me what brings you here.

Please tell me what's concerning you.

Please tell me what's the problem.

Please put me in the picture.

Where would you like to start?

You've been referred by _____. Now, how do you see your situation?

INFORMAL SETTINGS

Is there something on your mind?

I'm available if you want to talk.

You seem unhappy today (said sympathetically).

FOLLOW-UP 'LUBRICATING' COMMENTS

It's pretty hard to get started.

Take your time.

When you're ready.

Sometimes, you may need to complete organizational requirements for gathering basic information before giving helpees permission to talk. However, be flexible; for instance, helpees in crisis require psychological comfort before bureaucratic form filling, which can come later. On occasion, you may need to indicate the limitations of confidentiality surrounding the session, such as the need to report to a third party or any legal limitations. In addition, those of you who take notes may offer brief initial explanations for so doing and ask permission.

Some of you need to record helping sessions for supervision purposes. On many courses, helpees who see trainees under supervision know in advance that their sessions will be recorded. If this is not the case, permission to record will need to be sought right at the start of the session. Box 10.2 provides an example of requesting permission to record. In addition, good body and vocal messages can make it easier to obtain permission. Those of you who ask permission in nervous and hesitant ways are more likely to trigger doubts and resistances than those asking calmly and confidently.

BOX 10.2   EXAMPLE OF A REQUEST TO RECORD A SESSION

Would you mind if I video this session for supervision purposes? Only my supervisor [if relevant, add 'and supervision group'] will see the recording, which will be deleted when it has been reviewed. If you want, we can turn the recorder off at any time.

STRUCTURING SKILLS

Helping sessions are new experiences for many helpees. You can try to make the helping process more comprehensible and less threatening. Structuring entails explaining the helping process. You communicate structure by body, vocal and verbal messages. Here I just review structuring during the first part of helping, which may only last the first 10 to 15 minutes of an initial session. It is probably best to structure in two statements – an opening statement and a follow-up statement – rather than do it all at the beginning. If you offer the whole explanation at the beginning, you may fail to respond to helpees who want emotional release or are desperate to share information.

In two-part structuring, your opening statement provides the first occasion for structuring. Here you can establish time boundaries and give helpees permission to talk. After using your active listening skills to assist them to say why they have come, you may summarize the main points and check the accuracy of your summary. Then you can briefly and simply explain the remainder of the helping process. Box 10.3 presents two follow-up structuring statements providing a framework for the Relating–Understanding–Changing helping model presented in Chapter 6. The first statement is where the helpee clearly has only one main problem, and the second statement is where the helpee presents with more than one problem. If a specific situation has not already emerged, your follow-up statement requests the helpee to identify a situation within a main problem area for your work together.

BOX 10.3   EXAMPLES OF STRUCTURING STATEMENTS

OPENING OR FIRST STRUCTURING STATEMENT

We have about 45 minutes together, please tell me why you've come.

POSSIBLE SECOND STRUCTURING STATEMENTS

a) Single problem

You've given me some idea why you have come. Now since time is limited, I wonder if together we can select a specific situation within your problem (specify) that we can work on. I will help you to understand the situation more fully and then we can examine strategies for dealing better with it. Is that okay with you?

b) More than one problem

After summarizing the different problem areas, the helper says:

Which of these problems would you like to focus on? (The helpee states her or his choice.) Now I wonder if we can identify a particular situation within this problem that it is important for you to manage better. Then we can explore this situation more fully and perhaps come up with some useful strategies for dealing with it. Is that all right with you?

Structuring can strengthen collaborative relationships by establishing agendas or goals for the helping process as well as obtaining agreement on how to proceed. You may need to assist helpees choose a particular situation to work on that is important for them. You may also need to respond to questions. However, avoid allowing yourself to be lured into an intellectual discussion of the helping process. If you make structuring statements in a comfortable and confident way, most helpees will be happy to work within the suggested framework.

SUMMARIZING SKILLS

Summaries are brief helper statements about longer excerpts from helping sessions. Summaries pull together, clarify and reflect back different parts of a series of helpee statements during a discussion unit, at the end of a discussion unit, or at the beginning or end of helping sessions.

Here I focus on helper summaries at the start of helping. Where possible, they serve to move the session forwards. Such summaries may mirror back to helpees segments of what they have said; check and clarify understanding; or identify themes, problem areas and problem situations. Summaries may serve other purposes as well. If helpees have had a lengthy period of talking, you can summarize to establish your presence and make the helping conversation more two-way. Furthermore, if helpees tell their stories very rapidly, you can deliver summaries at a measured speech rate to calm them down.

When helpees tell why they have come for helping, you may use summaries that reflect whole units of communication. Such summaries tie together the main feelings and content of what they say. Basic reflection summaries serve a bridging function, enabling them to continue with the same topic or move on to another. Other functions include making sure you have listened accurately, rewarding them, and clarifying both of your understandings. A variation of the basic reflection summary is the reflecting feelings and reasons summary that links emotions with their perceived causes.

Another useful summarizing skill for early in helping is to be able to provide an overview of different problem areas. Imagine that a helpee comes to seek your assistance and starts describing a number of different problems. Identification of problem area summaries can provide them with clearer statements than they managed on their own. Furthermore, such summaries can provide a basis for asking them to prioritize which problem is most important and where they want to focus first. Box 10.4 provides examples of summarizing statements.

BOX 10.4   EXAMPLES OF SUMMARIES

BASIC REFLECTION SUMMARY

Helper to young woman

Your boyfriend has just left you and you have mixed feelings about this. You lived together for two years and it's a big adjustment being single again. You miss the good times you had together, but increasingly realize that they were getting fewer and fewer. You're hurt that he has left and yet you are starting to feel more optimistic about your future. You're not ready to go looking for another

(Continued)

(Continued)

boyfriend, but feel that you will when you have recovered emotionally. You do not want to rush into being with someone unsuitable. Have I heard you accurately?

IDENTIFICATION OF PROBLEM AREAS SUMMARY

Helper to middle-aged man

You have described at least four problem areas to me. First, your relationship with your wife, Susan, is not going as well as you would like. You're not enjoying each other as much as before and would like to become close again. Second, you are having difficulties with your 13-year-old son, Tim. He is getting increasingly outspoken and independent, yet you still care for him and want what is best for him. Third, after the recent death of your father, your mother – Emily – has started becoming very demanding and you want to deal better with her. Fourth, you feel stressed, have little in the way of non-work interests, and would like to lead a more balanced life. You no longer need to spend quite so much time working, but it's hard changing. Is that a fair summary?

Activity 10.1   Starting, structuring and summarizing skills

Work with a partner. Each of you thinks of a specific problem situation in your personal or work life that you are prepared to share in role-playing at the beginning of an initial session. Alternatively, you can role-play a helpee with a genuine problem situation. One of you acts as helpee. The helper conducts an interview of up to 15 minutes using the following skills:

- making an opening statement
- giving permission to talk
- paraphrasing
- reflecting feelings
- using small rewards
- using open-ended questions
- summarizing
- making a second structuring statement.

By the end of this beginning section of the session, the helper should have assisted the helpee in identifying a specific situation for your future work together.

   After completing the first part of an initial helping session, conduct a review together, possibly illustrated by going through a video or audio record of the session.

Then, after a suitable interval, partners can reverse roles.

ASKING QUESTIONS

CHAPTER GOALS

By studying and doing the activities in this chapter you should:

- Know about questions focusing on feelings and physical reactions, thinking, and communication and actions.
- Be introduced to interspersing active listening with questions.

This chapter focuses on asking questions mainly when helpees' problems have a large psychological component to them. There is a great danger that, when you question helpees, you revert to previous modes of relating and lose some, if not all, of your active listening skills. You should rein in tendencies to question too much and listen too little. In addition, you should be mindful that, if you can create a safe emotional climate, helpees will reveal more and deeper information, often without having to be asked.

Questions have the potential to damage helping relationships, sometimes beyond repair. Helpees can resent being interrogated from helpers' frames of reference rather than being understood from their own. For example, insufficiently skilled helpers may ask a series of questions, scarcely listen to the answers, and then go off on another tangent – whether or not helpees see this as relevant. In addition, helpees resent intrusive questioning about sensitive personal material. Furthermore, if clumsily taking control, you can create resistances and anger. Even when helpees appear acquiescent, you may encourage dependency rather than help them assume responsibility for their lives.

How do you go about assisting helpees to clarify and expand their understanding of problem situations? Without becoming too regimented, together you engage in a process of systematic inquiry about different aspects or 'angles' of a situation. However, when learning how to question, err on the side of asking too few rather than too many questions. Once you are more skilled at asking a few well-chosen questions within the context of collaborative relationships, then you can gradually build up the number of questions you ask, but never to the point where they control and de-power clients.

How you question is very important in addition to what you say. When questioning, you should use good vocal messages in terms of volume, articulation, pitch, emphasis and speech rate. For example, helpees may feel overwhelmed if your voice is loud and harsh. Furthermore, your body messages should clearly show attention and interest in helpees' answers. For instance, if you use little eye contact and have a stiff body posture, they may feel less inclined to answer questions well.

QUESTIONS ABOUT FEELINGS AND PHYSICAL REACTIONS

Questions can assist helpees in being specific about feelings and physical reactions. Frequently, since you cannot assume a common meaning, you need to clarify the labels that clients attach to feelings. For instance, follow-up questions to a helpee who says 'I am very depressed' might be: 'When you say you are very depressed, what exactly do you mean?' or 'When you say you are very depressed what are your specific feelings and physical reactions?' or 'You feel very depressed. Tell me more about that feeling?' Then you can collaborate with the helpee to identify the relevant feelings and physical reactions. Sometimes you may directly check out specific feelings or physical reactions: for instance, 'Do you feel suicidal sometimes?' or 'How is your appetite?'

Helpers often need to assist helpees in expanding and elaborating their feelings and physical reactions. Box 11.1 provides some illustrative questions.

BOX 11.1   EXAMPLES OF QUESTIONS THAT FOCUS ON FEELINGS AND PHYSICAL REACTIONS

When did you start feeling this way?

Tell me more about the feeling.

Describe how your body experiences the feeling.

Do you have any visual images that capture the feeling?

How has your mood been and how is it today?

Are there any other feelings that accompany or underlie that feeling?

How do you feel here and now?

How persistent is the feeling?

On a scale of 0 to 10 (or 0 to 100) how strong is the feeling?

QUESTIONS ABOUT THINKING

You can assist helpees to reveal their thoughts by asking appropriate questions. Sometimes you can access thinking from feelings, for instance, 'What thoughts preceded or accompanied those feelings?' On other occasions you may choose to access thinking from a helpee's or from another person's behaviour: for example, 'When you did that what were you thinking?' or 'When s/he said that what went through your mind?' You can also ask follow-up questions, such as 'Were there any other thoughts or images?'

Another way to look at thoughts is in terms of their strength. One way to do this is to label thoughts as cool, warm and hot. In particular, assist helpees to look out for hot thoughts that may trigger unwanted feelings and self-defeating communications. Often, helpees' thoughts about what other people are thinking can be the hot thoughts that drive their poor communication, for example, following the thought 'S/he is out to get me' with an angry outburst against them. Box 11.2 provides some illustrative questions focusing on helpees' thinking.

BOX 11.2 EXAMPLES OF QUESTIONS FOCUSING ON THINKING

What thoughts did you have before/during/after the situation?

What was going through your mind just before you started to feel this way?

What images do you get in the situation?

Go in slow motion through your thoughts in the situation.

How frequently do you get those thoughts?

When s/he acted like that what did you think?

Which of those thoughts is the hot thought?

What do you think s/he was thinking?

What are you afraid of?

What resources or strengths do you have in the situation?

What memories is this situation stirring up?

Were there any other thoughts or images?

In addition, helpers can ask specific questions about self-talk, rules and perceptions.

You can assist helpees to understand how they can think more deeply if you go beyond facts to search for their interpretations and perceptions. The information that helpees provide often has personal or symbolic meaning for them. For example, partners who do not receive flowers on their birthday may or may not think that this symbolizes lack of love. Questions that probe for personal meanings should be open and tentative, since helpees should know the answers better than anyone else, even if this does not always seem to be the case. Illustrative questions include: 'I'm wondering what the meaning of ____ is for you', 'What do you make of that?' and 'Why is ____ so important for you?'

QUESTIONS ABOUT COMMUNICATIONS AND ACTIONS

Questions about helpees' communication and actions aim to elicit specific details of how they behave. Often, helpees' reports are vague and they require assistance in becoming more specific. Sometimes helpers are poor at assisting them to discover what actually happened in situations and so the vagueness persists. Box 11.3 provides some examples of questions focusing on communication and actions.

BOX 11.3   EXAMPLES OF QUESTIONS FOCUSING ON COMMUNICATION AND ACTIONS

How did you behave?

What did you say?

How were you communicating with your voice?

How were you communicating with your body language?

How did s/he react when you did that (specify)?

What is the pattern of communication that develops between you when you row?

What happened before you did that?

What were the consequences of doing that?

When do you communicate that way?

Where do you act that way?

How many times a day/week/month do you ...?

How many minutes/hours do you ... each day?

A further question focusing on communications and actions is 'Show me?' You can invite helpees to illustrate the verbal, vocal and body messages they used in an interaction either on their own or in a role-play with you playing the other party. For instance, teachers who have difficulty with disciplining children can show you how they attempt to do this. Role-play allows the possibility of exploring patterns of communication that extend beyond an initial 'show me' response focused on just one unit of interaction. You can also record role-plays and play them back to helpees to illustrate points and develop helpees' skills of observing themselves.

INTERSPERSING ACTIVE LISTENING WITH QUESTIONS

Helpees feel interrogated when helpers ask a series of questions in quick succession. You can greatly soften your questioning if you pause to see if they wish to continue responding and then reflect each response. Interspersing active listening has the added advantage of ensuring that you check the accuracy of your understanding. Box 11.4 illustrates the process of interspersing active listening with questions. In this excerpt, the helper facilitates Oliver's description of his internal frame of reference, encouraging him to reveal his feelings and the reasons for them.

BOX 11.4   INTERSPERSING ACTIVE LISTENING WITH QUESTIONS

PROBLEM SITUATION

Oliver, an 18-year-old student, comes to his helper worried because he is not getting on with the other students in his dormitory.

INTERSPERSING ACTIVE LISTENING WITH QUESTIONS

Oliver: I'm very concerned that I am not getting on well with the students in my dormitory.

Helper: You're very worried about these relationships in the dorm. Can you tell me more?

Oliver: Yes, there are six of us and the others seem to be friends.

Helper: The others get on well, but how do they behave towards you?

Oliver: They are not openly nasty, but they do not seem to go out of their way to speak to me.

(Continued)

(Continued)

Helper: So you don't feel included, rather than they dislike you. Have I got you right?

Oliver: Yes.

Helper: And how do you behave towards them?

Oliver: I tend to keep to myself rather than try to talk with them. I seem to be afraid of them.

Always listen carefully to and respect what helpees have just said. Frequently, your next question can follow on from and encourage them to build upon their last response. Questioning that is logically linked to their responses creates a feeling of working together rather than of being directed by you. At the end of asking questions to clarify a problem situation, you can summarize the main points and check with the helpee about the accuracy and completeness of your summary.

Activity 11.1   Assessing and formulating questions

1 Look at Box 11.1:

   - Which questions do you think are really useful for probing helpees' feelings and physical reactions?
   - Can you think of other useful questions that you might ask for this purpose?

2 Look at Box 11.2:

   - Which questions do you think are really useful for probing helpees' thinking?
   - Can you think of other useful questions that you might ask for this purpose?

3 Look at Box 11.3:

   - Which questions do you think are really useful for probing helpees' communications and actions?
   - Can you think of other useful questions that you might ask for this purpose?

Activity 11.2   Interspersing active listening with questions

Work with a partner.

- Each partner picks a problem situation.
- Partner A acts as helper and partner B acts as helpee.

- Partner A spends 10 to 15 minutes interspersing questions with active listening as together s/he clarifies partner B's problem situation by asking questions about

  o feelings and physical reactions
  o thinking
  o communication and actions
  o anything else s/he considers relevant.

- At the end partner A summarizes the main details covered so far.
- Hold a sharing and feedback session.

Afterwards, if feasible, reverse roles and repeat the activity.

MONITORING

CHAPTER GOALS

By studying and doing the activities in this chapter you should:

- Learn about some ways helpees can monitor their feelings and physical reactions.
- Be introduced to ways helpees can monitor their thinking, communications and actions.

In addition to using active listening skills and asking questions, in some settings you can assist helpees to clarify problems by monitoring their feelings, physical reactions, thoughts and communications/actions. You may need to explain to them why the self-awareness gained by monitoring can be useful. Systematic monitoring can be important at the start of, during and after helping. At the outset, systematic monitoring can establish baselines and increase awareness. During helping, monitoring can serve to remind, check on progress and motivate. After helping, monitoring is relevant to maintaining gains, though helpees may not be so systematic in collecting information as during helping. Here I focus on monitoring at the start of helping.

MONITORING FEELINGS AND PHYSICAL REACTIONS

You can encourage helpees to monitor their feelings and physical reactions by using brief rating scales either daily or in terms of specific situations. Helpees can be asked to rate themselves on feelings such as mood (very happy to very depressed), anxiety level (no anxiety to very anxious), feelings of stress (no stress to very stressed) and so on. Common rating scales range from 0–10 or 0–100. You may need to train them in the skills of identifying and rating the key or important feelings and physical reactions they experience either daily or in situations. Below is an example of a simple scale that they can use to rate their level of anxiety either for each day or for specific situations.

No anxiety 0 1 2 3 4 5 6 7 8 9 10 **Extremely anxious**

You can also assist helpees to use worksheets to monitor and become more aware of how they feel in specific situations. Box 12.1 shows such a worksheet filled out in conjunction with a helpee who feels misunderstood by a friend. You may need to give helpees some practice in filling out such worksheets before asking them to complete them on their own.

BOX 12.1 WORKSHEET FOR IDENTIFYING AND RATING KEY PHYSICAL REACTIONS AND THOUGHTS IN A SITUATION

SITUATION

Who? What? When? Where?

Saturday, 7 pm, Medoo has a misunderstanding with her flatmate Gita.

KEY FEELING(S) AND PHYSICAL REACTION(S)

What did I feel? How did I physically react? Rating for each key feeling and physical reaction: 0–100%.

Angry 80%, Confused 60%, Hurt 65%.

THOUGHTS (PERCEPTIONS AND IMAGES)

What thoughts did I have just before I started to feel and physically react this way? Place a star by any hot thoughts.

However much I try, I just can't get through to Gita.

*I don't need this extra hassle from Gita on top of the pressure I already feel.

I've tried to be as reasonable as possible.

Normally Gita and I get on pretty well.

Gita does not think things through before speaking.

MONITORING THINKING

You can encourage helpees to monitor their thoughts, perceptions and images. Sometimes such monitoring is in conjunction with monitoring feelings and physical reactions as well (see Box 12.1). Helpees can be asked to put a star by any hot thoughts most associated with the feelings and physical reactions. Another approach to monitoring thoughts is to ask helpees to count every time they get a specific self-defeating thought, for instance 'I'm no good'. Counting can help them to become aware of the repetitive nature of their thinking. They may then record over a period of time the daily frequency of targeted thoughts and perceptions.

A further approach to monitoring thinking is to use the STC framework, which can be used by helpees and you alike as a tool for analysing how thoughts mediate between situations and how they feel, physically react, communicate and act about them. In this framework:

S = Situation (situations that helpees face)

T = Thoughts (thoughts and visual images)

C = Consequences (feelings, physical reactions, communications and actions).

The idea is that helpees do not go automatically from the situation (S) to the consequences of the situation (C). Instead the consequences (C) of the situation (S) are mediated by what and how they think (T). Their feelings, physical reactions, communications and actions, for good or ill, are mediated by their thoughts and mental processes.

Box 12.2 provides an STC worksheet that helpees can use both to monitor and analyse their thoughts in situations. You need to show them how to complete the worksheet. I have filled out the worksheet for Ruby, a 26-year-old who is very anxious about her first date with Tommy after ending her four-year relationship with Mike.

BOX 12.2   STC (SITUATION–THOUGHTS–CONSEQUENCES) WORKSHEET

SITUATION

State my problem situation clearly and succinctly

I'm having my first date with Tommy.

THOUGHTS

Record my thoughts about the situation

I must do very well. I've no idea how to make him like me. I am afraid that I will fail.

CONSEQUENCES

What are the consequences of my thoughts about the situation?

My feelings and physical reactions

Feelings: very anxious. Physical reactions: tension in my stomach, not concentrating properly.

My communications and actions

I'm talking too much about Mike and me. I'm not listening properly and showing enough interest in Tommy.

MONITORING COMMUNICATION AND ACTIONS

You can encourage helpees to monitor their behaviour and so become more aware of how they communicate and act in problem areas. Sometimes helpees agree to perform homework tasks, for instance telephoning to ask for a date and then recording how they behaved. The following are methods by which you can encourage helpees to monitor how they communicate and act.

DIARIES AND JOURNALS

Keeping a diary or journal is one way of monitoring communications and actions. Helpees can pay special attention to writing up critical incidents where they have used good or poor behaviours. Although diaries and journals may be useful, some helpees find this approach all too easy to ignore and too unsystematic.

FREQUENCY CHARTS

Frequency charts focus on how many times helpees enact a specific behaviour in a given time period, be it daily, weekly or monthly. For example, they may tally up how many cigarettes they smoke in a day and then transfer this information to a monthly chart broken down by days. Another example is that of unemployed Annie, who agrees with her employment counsellor to record, each day for a week, her job search behaviours on a Job Search Activity Chart. The chart lists activities on the horizontal axis and days on the vertical axis. The activities listed on the horizontal axis are written application, phone application, letter enquiry, phone enquiry, cold canvass, approach to contact, employment centre visit, and interview attended. The counsellor instructs Annie to write the number 1 in the relevant box each time she performs an action.

SITUATION, THOUGHTS AND CONSEQUENCES (STC) LOGS

Filling in the three-column situation, thoughts and consequences (STC) logs or worksheets can assist helpees to see the connections between how they thought and how they felt, physically reacted, and communicated or acted. See Box 12.2 for an example.

VERBAL, VOCAL AND BODY MESSAGE LOGS

Frequently helpees possess a low awareness of their vocal and body communication. During the understanding stage, you and your helpees may become aware of some areas important for understanding helpees' problem situations. For instance, a helper works with Bill, married with three children, whose problem situations centre around his difficulty setting limits on his widowed mother, Meryl, who makes repeated telephone and face-to-face requests for time and attention, even though she is well able to look after herself. Box 12.3 shows a log to collect information about how Bill communicates in these situations. Bill is cued in advance to observe specific verbal, vocal and body messages.

BOX 12.3   EXAMPLE OF VERBAL, VOCAL AND BODY MESSAGES LOG

	How I communicated		
Situation	Verbal messages	Vocal messages	Body messages
1			
2			
(and so on)			

ASSISTING HELPEES TO MONITOR

Helpees are not in the habit of systematically recording observations about how they feel, physically react, think and communicate/act. You may need to motivate them to do so. For instance, you could explain to Bill, 'Systematically writing down how you communicate with your words, voice and body each time your mother attempts to get you to spend time with her provides us with information to develop useful strategies for setting limits on her requesting time and attention behaviour.'

Always either supply monitoring logs or supervise helpees in setting up the format for a log. Do not expect them to make logs on their own. They may not do so in the first place and, if they do, they may get them wrong.

Helpees are not naturally accurate self-observers. Consequently, you may need to train them in discriminating and recording specific behaviours. They require clarity not only about what to record, but also about how to record it. In addition, they require an awareness of any tendencies they have to misperceive or selectively perceive their actions, for instance, being more inclined to notice weaknesses than strengths.

Reward helpees with interest and praise when they fill in logs. This guide-line is based on the basic behavioural principle that actions that are rewarding are more likely to be repeated. Furthermore, always reward helpees for their efforts by debriefing them. Encourage them to use information they record on monitoring logs for self-exploration and evaluation. Without doing their work for them, help them to understand the meaning of the information they have collected.

Activity 12.1   Monitoring feelings, physical reactions and thoughts

Role-play helping a partner who acts as a 'helpee' and has a specific situation in which s/he is experiencing feelings and physical reactions that may be self-defeating. Offer reasons to your helpee for monitoring their feelings, physical reactions and thoughts. Using the format of Box 12.1, help them to identify key feelings, physical reactions and thoughts in the situation.

Afterwards hold a feedback and discussion session. Then, if appropriate, reverse roles.

Activity 12.2   Monitoring situations, thoughts and consequences

Role-play helping a partner who acts as a 'helpee' and has a specific situation in which s/he is behaving in a self-defeating manner. Offer reasons to your helpee for monitoring to discover the relationship between their thoughts, feelings and communications/actions. Using the STC format of Box 12.2, help your helpee to describe the situation and to identify their thinking, and its feelings/physical reactions and communication/actions consequences.

Afterwards hold a feedback and discussion session. Then, if appropriate, reverse roles.

Activity 12.3   Monitoring verbal, vocal and body messages

Role-play helping a partner who acts as a 'helpee' and has a specific situation in which s/he either is or may be communicating poorly. Offer reasons to your helpee for monitoring their communication in the situation. Then, using the format of the log in Box 12.3, train your helpee to observe and record systematically their verbal, vocal and body messages in the situation.

Afterwards hold a feedback and discussion session. Then, if appropriate, reverse roles.

OFFERING CHALLENGES AND FEEDBACK  13

CHAPTER GOALS

By studying and doing the activities in this chapter you should:

- Gain some knowledge and skills for offering challenges.
- Learn about how to offer both observational and experiential feedback.

This chapter differs from previous chapters in that the skills of offering challenges and offering feedback represent responses more clearly emanating from the helper's external frame of reference than designed to clarify the helpee's internal frame of reference. The starting point of any good collaborative relationship is to use active listening and asking questions skills to understand and clarify the helpee's frame of reference. Offering challenges and offering feedback are two skills that you can use that go beyond clarifying helpees' existing frames of reference to expand how they view themselves and their problems.

OFFERING CHALLENGES

Challenging is perhaps a more gentle word than confronting, which conjures up images of helpees sitting in hot seats having their self-protective habits remorselessly stripped away by aggressive helpers. Challenges come from your external frame of reference, with the aim of aiding helpees to develop new and better perspectives about themselves, others and their problem situations. Skilled challenges invite helpees to examine discrepancies in their feelings, thoughts and communications about which, for various reasons, they remain insufficiently aware. The challenges I advocate here have two distinctive characteristics: first, they tend to be fairly close to helpees' existing internal frames of reference; and second, they are given in a relatively non-threatening manner. As Box 13.1 illustrates, challenges can come in many shapes and sizes.

BOX 13.1   EXAMPLES OF CHALLENGING INCONSISTENCIES

Inconsistency between verbal, vocal and/or body messages:
You're telling me you feel sad about it, yet you are smiling.

Inconsistency between words and actions:
You say that you are through with him, yet you keep phoning him.

Inconsistency between values and actions:
You say that you value honesty, but you also don't mind bending the truth sometimes.

Inconsistency between giving and keeping one's word:
You said that you would spend more time with your children, but do not seem to have done so.

Inconsistency between earlier and present statements:
Last session you said you were fed up with your boss, but now you're saying she's pretty good really.

Inconsistency between statements and evidence:
You've said that your partner never does anything for you, and now you're telling me that he washed up after dinner last night.

Inconsistency between own and others' evaluations:
I'm getting two messages. You seem to think that you handled the situation okay, but the rest of the group is still unhappy with your behaviour.

HOW TO OFFER CHALLENGES

Verbal messages for offering challenges include: 'On the one hand ... on the other ...', 'On the one hand ... but ...', 'You say ... but ...', and 'I'm getting two messages ...' or 'I'm getting a mixed message ...'. Your vocal and body messages should remain relaxed and friendly. When starting, restrict yourself to offering no more than mildly threatening challenges to helpees, because of the huge potential for helping relationships to turn sour when inexperienced helpers make strong challenges.

When challenging it is important to keep helpees' ears open to the new information. Therefore offer challenges as an equal, avoid talking down, and always remember that challenges are invitations for exploration. A major risk in challenging helpees is that they perceive what you say as put-downs.

Use a minimum amount of 'muscle', only offering challenges as strongly as your goals require. Strong challenges can create resistances. Although sometimes necessary, even with skilled helpers such challenges are generally best avoided. This is especially so early in helping relationships when rapport and trust are not yet established. Strategies that helpees can use to resist challenges include discrediting challengers, persuading challengers to change their views, devaluing the issue, seeking support elsewhere for views being challenged, and agreeing with the challenge inside helping but then doing nothing about it outside.

Leave the ultimate responsibility for assessing the value of your challenges with helpees, who can then decide whether they actually help them to move forwards in their exploration. Often challenges are only mildly discrepant to helpees' existing perceptions. If well timed and tactfully worded, such challenges are unlikely to elicit a high degree of defensiveness.

Last, be careful not to overdo offering challenges. Nobody likes being persistently challenged. With constant challenges you create an unsafe emotional climate. If you offer challenges skilfully, you can assist helpees to enlarge their understanding and act more effectively. However, if you challenge too often and too clumsily you can block them from achieving insight and undermine the creation of a good collaborative relationship.

OFFERING FEEDBACK

Offering feedback skills and offering challenges skills overlap. However, challenging skills are used in response to helpees' inconsistencies, whereas there is no assumption of inconsistency in this section on offering feedback skills. Here I distinguish between observational feedback, 'I observe you as ...', and experiential feedback, 'I experience you as ...'.

OBSERVATIONAL FEEDBACK

Helpers as observers of helpees' communication may see it differently and possibly more accurately than helpees perceive it themselves. When you and your helpees are truly collaborating to try to understand their problems and problem situations, there may be occasions where you may decide to offer feedback based on your own observations. Take helpees who have just shown you how they communicate in specific situations. After mini-role-plays, helpees may show some insight into their verbal, vocal and body messages. However, as an observer, you may wish to bring something else to their attention.

How do you go about offering feedback? Box 13.2 makes many suggestions for going about this task. These suggestions include: using 'I' messages; being specific and, where possible, stating feedback in the positive; using confirmatory as well as corrective feedback; considering demonstrating feedback; and providing opportunities for helpees to respond to feedback.

BOX 13.2   GUIDELINES FOR OFFERING FEEDBACK

USE 'I' MESSAGES RATHER THAN 'YOU' MESSAGES

'You' message

You did ...

'I' message

I experienced you as ...

BE SPECIFIC AND, WHERE POSSIBLE, STATE FEEDBACK IN THE POSITIVE

Non-specific and negative

That was poor.

Specific and positive

I thought you could speak with a louder voice and use more eye contact.

USE CONFIRMATORY AS WELL AS CORRECTIVE FEEDBACK

I thought the loudness of your voice was good, but that you could still use more eye contact.

CONSIDER EMOTIONAL AS WELL AS BEHAVIOURAL FEEDBACK

When you spoke with a loud voice and made very direct eye contact, I felt overpowered by you.

CONSIDER DEMONSTRATING FEEDBACK

I would like to show you how your eye contact came over to me ... (then demonstrate).

PROVIDE OPPORTUNITIES FOR HELPEES TO RESPOND TO FEEDBACK

What's your reaction to what I've just said?

After conducting mini-role-plays, my preference is to ask helpees to evaluate themselves before offering any feedback. Reasons for doing this include encouraging them to participate actively and reducing the need for feedback from me since they may have noticed my points anyway. Further reasons are to build helpees' skills of self-observation and to increase the likelihood of their being receptive to my feedback because they have already been given the opportunity to assess themselves. For instance, after inviting them to comment on their performance and listening to their responses, I might summarize what they have said, enquire 'Would you mind if I make one or two observations …?', and then, if given permission, succinctly offer my feedback.

EXPERIENTIAL FEEDBACK

Feedback can also involve you in using your experiencing of helpees as a springboard for offering observations about both the helpee and the helping process. To an extent helping sessions and contacts can be microcosms of outside life. Helpees can bring into them the same patterns of communication that create difficulties for them outside helping. However, you should be very careful not to let your own personal unfinished business interfere with how you experience helpees.

Instances where your experiencing of helpees' interpersonal style may throw light on their problems outside include not arriving on time for interviews, speaking in distant ways, and seeking reassurance. For instance, with a helpee who continually seeks reassurance, you might comment: 'I feel put on the spot because I experience pressure from you for reassurance, whereas I'd like to encourage you to rely on your own judgment.' Giving positive experiential feedback to helpees with low self-esteem can sometimes be useful: for example, 'I experience you as having some strength to deal with the situation' or 'I experience you as having much to offer a friend'. Such comments need to be genuine feedback rather than superficial reassurance.

You can also offer experiential feedback concerning the helping process. For example, if helpees repetitively go over the same ground, you might say: 'I experience you as having taken that topic as far as you can go at the moment and it might be profitable to move on. What do you think?' Another example is that of sharing how you experience a helpee who uses humour as a distancing device whenever topics become too personal. For instance, you could comment: 'I get the sense that this topic is getting too close for comfort and so you're starting to act the clown to avoid dealing with it directly.' Needless to say, tact and good timing are very important if helpees are to use such experiential feedback to move forwards rather than backwards.

Activity 13.1   Offering challenges skills

1 What does the concept of offering challenges to helpees mean to you? Early in a helping relationship, what are the advantages and disadvantages of offering challenges to helpees?
2 Using Box 13.1 as a guide, formulate a challenging response in each of the following areas:

- inconsistency between verbal, vocal and/or body messages
- inconsistency between words and actions
- inconsistency between values and actions
- inconsistency between giving and keeping one's word
- inconsistency between earlier and present statements
- inconsistency between statements and evidence
- inconsistency between own and others' evaluations.

Activity 13.2   Offering feedback skills

1 Refer to the guidelines for offering feedback in Box 13.2 and formulate statements for illustrating each of the different guidelines.
2 Work in a pair, with partner A as 'helpee' and partner B as 'helper'.

- Partner A selects a problem situation involving another person where s/he thinks they might communicate better.
- Partners A and B conduct a mini-role-play in which partner B plays this other person and partner A demonstrates how s/he currently communicates in the situation.
- Afterwards, partner B invites partner A to comment on her/his verbal, vocal and body messages in the situation.
- Then partner B gives observational feedback to partner A.
- Next, hold a sharing and discussion session about partner A's offering observational feedback skills.
- Then, if appropriate, reverse roles.

3 What does the concept of offering experiential feedback mean to you?
4 Formulate one or more offering experiential feedback statements.

SELF-DISCLOSING

CHAPTER GOALS

By studying and doing the activities in this chapter you should:

- Learn about different kinds of challenges and how to offer them.
- Start knowing about offering both observational and experiential feedback and how to do so.

Helpers relate to helpees in numerous settings, formal and informal, and where helping may or may not be a part of other primary roles. Unlike in formal counselling and psychotherapy, helpers who use basic counselling skills are often already in dual relationships with helpees: for example, supervisor–worker, speech therapist–patient, or hotel manager–guest. Since it is impossible to generalize for every helping context, this chapter focuses on helping contacts where psychological agendas predominate for helpees. Should you talk about yourself at all when working with helpees? How can you show genuineness and humanity if you present as blank screens to helpees? Helper self-disclosure relates to the ways in which you let yourself be known to helpees.

Helper self-disclosure, even in brief helping contacts, can be for good or ill. Possible positive consequences from talking about yourself include providing new insights and perspectives, demonstrating a useful skill, equalizing and humanizing the helping relationship, normalizing helpees' difficulties, instilling hope, and offering reassurance. There are, however, grave dangers in inappropriately talking about yourself. For example, you may hijack the focus of the helping conversation to yourself and burden helpees with your problems. Furthermore, you may come across as weak and unstable when vulnerable helpees want a helper who has 'got their act together'.

Usually the term self-disclosure refers to face-to-face intentional verbal disclosure. However, there are numerous other ways in which you can disclose, including your vocal and body messages, your availability, office decor, phone, written or e-mail communications, and size of fees! A useful distinction exists between self-involving responses and self-disclosing responses. Another way of stating this is that there are at least two major dimensions of helper self-disclosure: showing involvement and disclosing personal information.

SHOWING INVOLVEMENT

There is a story about a psychoanalyst who would go down to the coffee shop leaving her cassette recorder on in the consulting room to listen to her patients' free associations and dreams. One day a patient, who was meant to be on the couch, came into the coffee shop, and the following dialogue took place.

Psychoanalyst: What are you doing down here? You're meant to be in psychoanalysis.

Patient: Don't worry, Doc. I've left my cassette player on up there speaking into your cassette recorder.

Unlike this caricature of a totally detached psychoanalyst, you can show involvement to assist the helping process. Disclosures that show involvement can humanize helping so that helpees feel that they are relating to real people. There is a 'here-and-now' quality in showing involvement by sharing reactions to helpees. Three areas for disclosing involvement are responding to specific helpee disclosures, responding to helpees as people, and responding to helpees' vulnerability. Box 14.1 provides examples of helper statements for each area.

BOX 14.1   EXAMPLES OF DISCLOSURES SHOWING INVOLVEMENT

RESPONDING TO SPECIFIC DISCLOSURES

I'm really pleased.

That's awful.

That's good.

I'm sorry to hear that.

RESPONDING TO HELPEES AS PEOPLE

I admire your persistence.

I appreciate your intelligence.

RESPONDING TO HELPEES' VULNERABILITY

I'm available if you get really anxious.

I feel sad for you when you are so unhappy.

DISCLOSING PERSONAL INFORMATION

Disclosure of personal information may be either initiated by helpers or in response to helpees' questions. One area of disclosing personal information relates to your qualifications and experience. Sometimes this information is already available, but if not you need to decide what and how much to reveal. When asked about your qualifications and experience, there is much to be said for honest but brief answers.

Another area about revealing personal information relates to details of your private life and outside interests. Since helping settings range from the very informal to the very formal, the appropriateness of degrees of disclosure about your private life may differ greatly from one setting to another. For example, in peer helping, it can be part of the original contract that each party discusses problems in their private lives. In some informal settings, such as youth centres, helpers may selectively reveal details of their private lives and interests as part of the relationship-building process with their clientele. For example, youth workers with interests in certain sporting activities and pop music might well want to share these interests when conversing with groups of young people. However, when assisting individuals, disclosing such personal information could, but not necessarily would, be less appropriate. In instances where helping takes place in conjunction with many other primary roles, such as doctor, welfare officer or priest, helpers may be less likely to disclose details of their private lives and interests.

Sometimes your previous or present experiences in your personal and working lives are similar to those currently experienced by helpees. Helpers who disclose personal information about similar experiences can assist helpees to feel that they understand what they are going through. For instance, people anxious about exams might feel differently about helpers who share that they too have been similarly anxious. Additionally, such disclosures can make it easier for helpees to talk about their own experiences. Box 14.2 contains an example of the disclosure of personal information that strengthens the collaborative relationship.

BOX 14.2 EXAMPLE OF DISCLOSING PERSONAL INFORMATION

Helper: Khalid, as you've been talking of your difficulties over taking exams, it reminds me of a period in my life when I was really scared about exams and had to do something about it. Though clearly our experiences differ, I think I do have some idea of what you're going through.

Khalid: Thanks for that. One of the hardest things about being so scared is feeling so awfully alone and useless. It's as if I'm burdening and boring people by talking about it.

In some types of helping, disclosure of shared experiences is a mandatory part of the process; for instance, striving for honesty in owning up to your addiction is integral to Alcoholics Anonymous and some drug addiction programmes. Furthermore, in such programmes there are also testimonials by those who are no longer drinking or taking drugs. Such personal information disclosures provide evidence that, even though it may involve an agonizing struggle, people can be successful in containing their addictions.

Assuming you consider self-disclosure of personal information appropriate, you have many choices in how you do this. One choice is whether to restrict yourself to past experiences or discuss current experiences. Another choice is that of how honest to be or how much detail to share. A further choice is that of whether to go beyond disclosing facts to disclosing feelings – for instance, not only having been unemployed, but then having to struggle against feelings of depression and uselessness. Additional choices include revealing how you coped with your experiences and how you feel about them now. In the kind of brief helping assumed by the Relating–Understanding–Changing helping process model, you will not have the opportunity to develop the 'relational depth' that counsellors and psychotherapists achieve with some helpees in a longer series of helping sessions.

Below are some guidelines concerning appropriate disclosure of personal information where your experiences are similar to those of helpees.

1   *Talk about yourself*   In general, avoid disclosing the experience of third parties whom you either know or have heard about.
2   *Talk about past experiences*   A risk of disclosing current experiences, such as going through a divorce, is that you have insufficient emotional distance to ensure that your own agendas do not become intermingled with those of helpees.
3   *Be to the point*   You should avoid slowing down or defocusing the helping through lack of relevance or talking too much.
4   *Use good vocal and body messages*   You need to be genuine and consistent, with vocal and body messages matching your verbal disclosures.
5   *Be sensitive to helpees' reactions*   You should possess sufficient awareness to realize when your disclosures might be helpful and when they might be unwelcome or a burden.
6   *Be sensitive to helper–helpee differences*   Expectations of helpers differ across cultures, social class, race and gender, and so do expectations regarding appropriateness of helper self-disclosure.
7   *Share personal experiences sparingly*   Be very careful not to switch the focus of helping from the helpee to yourself.
8   *Beware of counter-transference*   Counter-transference refers to negative and positive feelings towards helpees based on unresolved areas in helpers' own lives. Intentionally or unintentionally, some helpers disclose personal information to manipulate helpees to meet unfulfilled needs for approval, intimacy and sex. This possibility highlights the importance of being aware of your motivation and behaving ethically.

Activity 14.1   Showing involvement

1 With respect to your present or future helping work, write down the sorts of situations in which it might be appropriate for you to show involvement to helpees early on in helping.
2 Using Box 14.1 as a guide, formulate one or more showing involvement disclosures in each of the following areas:

   - responding to specific helpee disclosures
   - responding to helpees as people
   - responding to helpees' vulnerability.

3 Work with a partner and use basic counselling skills to help her/him to discuss a personal concern or to role-play a helpee. During the course of a mini-session, try, on a few occasions, to make disclosures showing involvement. Afterwards your partner gives you feedback on the impact of your showing involvement disclosures. Then reverse roles.

Activity 14.2   Disclosing personal information

1 With regard to your present or future helping work, write down the sorts of situations in which it might be appropriate for you to share personal information with helpees early on in helping.
2 For each situation formulate one or more disclosing personal information responses.
3 Work with a partner and use basic counselling skills to help her/him to discuss a personal concern or to role-play being a helpee. During the course of a mini-session, try, at one or more appropriate occasions, to disclose personal information. Afterwards your partner gives you feedback on the impact of your personal information disclosures. Then reverse roles.

MANAGING RESISTANCES AND MAKING REFERRALS

CHAPTER GOALS

By studying and doing the activities in this chapter you should:

- Know some different ways of managing resistances.
- Learn about when and how to make referrals and recommendations.

This chapter on managing resistances and making referrals concerns two areas that can create difficulties for helpers. Many of you will see helpees who have been referred by others and have not come of their own free will. Furthermore, when helping starts, helpees can still resist participating fully in collaborative relationships. In addition, in some instances you may consider that you are not the right person to help someone and that another might do the job better. This raises the issue of whether and how to refer or recommend that helpees go elsewhere.

MANAGING RESISTANCES

Resistances may be broadly defined as anything that gets in the way of helping. Resistances are helpees' feelings, thoughts and communications that frustrate, impede, slow down and sometimes stop the helping process. Reluctance, which is unwillingness or disinclination on the part of potential or actual helpees to enter into the helping process, is an aspect of being resistant. Some helpees do not see the need for help. They may reluctantly see you to meet others' wishes: for instance, children sent by teachers or parents, or substance abusers and perpetrators of domestic violence sent by the courts. Many helpees are ambivalent about discussing their problems. At the same time as wanting change, they may have anxieties about changing from their safe and known ways and also about the helping process, for instance, revealing personal information. Furthermore, helpees may resist those of you whose behaviour is too discrepant from their expectations or from what they think they need.

HOW TO MANAGE RESISTANCES

The following are some suggestions for understanding and dealing with resistances early on in helping. Many of these skills are also relevant for later sessions and contacts. Because there are so many variations and reasons for resistances within the broad range of contexts in which helpers use basic counselling skills, it is impossible to cover all contingencies.

USE ACTIVE LISTENING SKILLS

Helpers may wrongly attribute the sources of helpees' resistances and be too quick to blame them for lack of cooperation and progress. Beginning – and even more experienced – helpers may both sustain and create resistances through poor listening skills. Resistances are a normal part of the early stages of helping. By using good active listening skills, you do much to build the trust needed to lower resistances. Some helpees' resistances manifest themselves in aggression. Then, rather than feeling the need to justify yourself and become sucked into a competitive contest, one approach to handling such aggression is to reflect it back, locating the feelings clearly in the helpee, but indicate that you have picked up their anger loud and clear. Where helpees provide reasons for their hostility, you can reflect these too. Just showing helpees that you understand their internal frame of reference, especially if done consistently, can diminish resistances.

JOIN WITH CLIENTS

Sometimes helpers can lower helpees' resistances by helping them feel that they have a friend at court. For instance, you can initially listen and offer support to spouses expressing resentment about partners.

> *Sachin:* I'm not sure I should be coming because I think Jessica should be seeing you. She's the one who is causing the problems and is really screwed up.
>
> *Helper:* You feel uncertain about being here because you think Jessica should really come, since she's the person causing the difficulties.
>
> *Sachin:* Yeah (and then proceeds to share his side of the story).

In the above instance the helper accepted Sachin's focus on Jessica's deficiencies and used his need to mention these to build the helping relationship. Were the helpee to continue to complain about his partner, after an appropriate period of time the helper might have built up enough trust and goodwill either for Sachin to focus on his own behaviour of his own accord or for the helper to assist him to make this switch.

GIVE PERMISSION TO DISCUSS RELUCTANCE AND FEARS

If as a helper you receive overt or subtle messages from helpees that they have reservations about your seeing them, you can bring the agenda out into the open and give them permission to elaborate. In the following example, a parole officer responds to a juvenile delinquent's seeming reluctance to disclose anything significant.

> *Parole officer:*   I detect you are unwilling to open up to me because I'm your parole officer. If I'm right, I'm wondering what specifically worries you about that?

Where appropriate, you can also give helpees permission to discuss differences in helper–helpee characteristics, for instance culture and race, that can make it harder for some to participate in helping.

INVITE COOPERATION

Establishing good collaborative relationships with helpees both prevents and also overcomes many resistances. You can make statements early on in the helping process that can aim to create the idea of a partnership, a shared endeavour in which you work together to assist helpees to deal with their problems and thus lead happier and more fulfilled lives.

ENLIST SELF-INTEREST

You can assist helpees to identify reasons or gains for them of participating in helping. For instance, you can assist children who perceive their parents as picking on them, and as the ones with problems, to see that they themselves might be happier with better skills for coping with their parents. Furthermore, questions that challenge helpees with the adequacy of their own behaviour may enlist self-interest. Such questions include 'Where is your current behaviour getting you?' and 'How is that behaviour helping you?' Questions that encourage helpees to think about goals are also useful, for example, 'What are your goals in the situation?' and 'Wouldn't you like to be more in control of your life?'

REWARD SILENT HELPEES FOR TALKING

Some helpees find it difficult to talk, whether or not they are with helpers. Others may find it particularly difficult to talk to helpers. Without coming on too strong, you can respond more frequently and more obviously. For example, you may use more small rewards when helpees talk.

In addition, you can offer encouragement by reflecting and making the most of what they say. Furthermore, you can reflect the difficulty certain helpees have in talking, even though they may not have verbalized this themselves.

MAKING REFERRALS AND RECOMMENDATIONS

Early on in helping and also later, you may face decisions about referring or recommending that helpees go elsewhere. Even experienced counsellors have types of helpees with whom they feel more competent and comfortable and others less so. Noted psychotherapist Arnold Lazarus stated that an important helping principle is to 'Know your limitations and other clinicians' strengths'. Referrals and recommendations should be made where other helpers have skills that you do not possess or more appropriate personal styles for particular helpees. Important ethical issues surround referral, especially where other helpers have more expertise with specific problems, for instance with substance abuse or unwanted pregnancy.

Referral or recommendation may not be an either/or matter. Sometimes you may continue working with helpees but also refer them to other helping professionals. Alternatively, you may be the recipients of referrals from other helping professionals who continue working with the same helpee. Sometimes you can refer helpees to gain additional knowledge about their problems. For example, consider referring helpees with concentration blocks, or difficulty performing sexually, for medical checks. Then, depending on the outcome of these checks, you have relevant information about whether or not to continue seeing them, either alone or in conjunction with a physician, or not at all.

On many occasions you can refer the helpee's problems rather than the helpee her/himself to others. For example, you can discuss with colleagues or supervisors how best to assist certain helpees. Occasions when you may refer helpees' problems rather than helpees include when you are the only helper available in an area, when helpees state a clear preference for continuing working with you, and when they are unlikely to follow through on referrals.

HOW TO REFER

The following are some considerations and skills for making referrals and recommendations. You may be too ready to refer helpees and should avoid doing so unnecessarily. Sometimes it is better for helpees to continue working with you. If under-confident you should tune into your anxieties and fears about seeing certain helpees. Then you can endeavour to build your confidence and skills to expand the range of helpees with whom you can work. Wherever possible, ensure that you have adequate supervision and support.

As time goes by you should try to develop a good feel for your strengths and limitations. You should be realistic about the kinds of helpees with whom you work well and those with whom you are less skilled. You also need to be realistic about your workload and set appropriate limits on it.

Good referrals and recommendations are more likely to be made to people whom you know and trust, rather than done 'blind'. Get to know the relevant resources available in your location so that you can avoid recommending that helpees go to helpers about whose competence you are unsure. In addition, even if you know the other helpers, it may still be wise to check if they have time available for seeing new helpees.

Where possible, make referrals and recommendations early on. If you defer referrals longer than necessary, you waste helpees' and your own time. Furthermore, it is preferable to refer helpees before they emotionally bond with you.

When making referrals and recommendations, calmly explain why this may be a good idea. You should be able to support your explanation from information already revealed by helpees. It is important that helpees are absolutely clear about how to make contact with the other helpers. You can hand out other helpers' business cards or write down addresses and phone numbers.

Be prepared to spend time discussing any queries and emotional reactions helpees may have to your recommendations. If they are in crisis, you may need to accompany them to the other helper's office. Another consideration is whether and what information you should provide for the next or a different helper. You can discuss such issues with helpees and, if necessary, ask permission to share information.

Last, you should build your support network. Support networks provide professional support when you want to refer problems rather than people. They are likely to overlap with referral networks, but some members' roles are different. For example, you can gain support by discussing helpees' problems with supervisors and trainers, but you are less likely to refer helpees to them.

Activity 15.1   Managing resistances

1   For a helping setting in which you either work or might work, list the main ways helpees might show resistances early on in helping.
2   Formulate the following kinds of managing resistances responses:

- joining responses
- permission to discuss reluctance and fears responses
- enlisting client self-interest responses.

Activity 15.2   Making referrals

In regard to either your current or future helping work:

1 When might you refer helpees to other helpers?
2 What categories of helpers do you require in your referral network?
3 What categories of helpers do you require in your support network – when you refer problems but not helpees?
4 What are some considerations in making good referrals?
5 When might you be at risk of making unnecessary referrals?

FACILITATING PROBLEM SOLVING

CHAPTER GOALS

By studying and doing the activity in this chapter you should:

* Know ways to assist helpees in clarifying their goals.
* Develop skills for getting helpees to generate and explore options.
* Start being able to assist helpees in planning.

Though a simplification, in Chapter 6 I mentioned that facilitating problem solving and improving communications/actions and thoughts are two approaches that helpers and helpees can take when addressing issues of change. To some extent the two approaches overlap. In the facilitating problem-solving approach, you stay close to helpees' internal frames of reference and mainly draw upon their suggestions for change. In the improving communications/actions and thoughts approach, you are more active in working with helpees to specify the behaviours requiring improvement, and in helping them to achieve this end.

The facilitating problem-solving approach, the focus of the present chapter, is not restricted to beginning helpers. Experienced helpers, too, need to be very skilled at combining active listening skills with probes designed to assist helpees to clarify goals, explore options for attaining them, and develop plans to implement a chosen option.

CLARIFYING GOALS

When some helpees, with the assistance of their helpers, have clarified their understanding of the key dimensions of their problems and problem situations, of their own accord they then clarify goals and proceed to attain them. You use good active listening skills to facilitate them to tap into their own resources and act appropriately in problem situations. The main thrust of Carl Rogers' person-centred approach to counselling and helping is that helpers should provide the facilitative conditions and emotional climate so that helpees can get in touch with what they truly feel as a basis for taking effective action in their lives. You should be sensitive to the extent that helpees just want you to be there as a skilled listener while they do their own work.

On other occasions, you can follow up summaries that pull together the main dimensions of problem situations with questions that assist helpees to clarify their goals in dealing with them. When first meeting helpers, some helpees are so overwhelmed that they lose sight of what they really want to achieve. As time goes by, many will have calmed down sufficiently so that they can think fairly rationally about their goals. However, they may still require assistance from you to articulate these goals.

You might start assisting helpees to address issues of change with a structuring statement along the lines of 'Now we have clarified and summarized many of the main dimensions of your problem situation, perhaps we can now try and clarify your goals in it. Do you think this would be helpful?' Many helpees will answer 'yes' right away. Some might answer 'What do you mean?' If so, you can tactfully explain that clarifying where you want to go makes it easier to decide how to get there.

You can distinguish between outcome goals, 'Where do I want to go?', and process goals, 'What are my sub-goals or steps in getting where I want to go?' Here I focus on outcome goals. Often, when practising as a counselling psychologist, I have found that helpees start by being insufficiently creative when thinking about goals for specific situations. Rather than latch on to the first goal that comes to mind, you can assist them to generate and consider a range of goals by asking 'What are your options in setting goals?' Such goals can be both positive, 'What do I want to achieve?', and negative, 'What do I want to avoid?', and are often a mixture of the two. Box 16.1 lists some questions that helpers can use to assist helpees in clarifying their goals in problem situations.

BOX 16.1 SOME QUESTIONS FOR CLARIFYING GOALS

- What are your goals in the situation?
- What would you consider a successful outcome?
- What are your options in setting goals?
- What do you want to achieve in the situation?

    o for yourself
    o for one or more others
    o for your relationship, if appropriate.

- What do you want to avoid in the situation?

    o for yourself
    o for one or more others
    o for your relationship, if appropriate.

Avoid bombarding helpees with questions about goals. In most instances, small is beautiful. A few well-chosen questions that get to the heart of what they want to achieve and avoid are all that is necessary. However, sometimes you may need to facilitate them in exploring deeper goals and the values that underpin them, rather than surface goals. In all instances, you should respect helpees' rights to set their own goals and also intersperse active listening with questions to clarify goals.

GENERATING AND EXPLORING OPTIONS

Questions that clarify goals are about ends. Questions for generating and exploring options are about the means to achieve the ends. Just as helpees can latch on to the first goal that comes to mind, so they can latch on to the first method of achieving a goal that comes into their heads.

Box 16.2 is a case example that highlights the outcomes of using generating and exploring options questions to assist helpees to attain goals. Often, once helpees set goals, they feel stuck and do not know how to proceed. Skilled questioning to help them to generate and explore options assists them to put on their thinking caps and use their minds creatively. Many helpees are wiser than they know, but have insufficient confidence and skills to get their wisdom out into the open.

You may need to assist helpees to think about the consequences of options. Often it is best to generate options first and assess consequences afterwards. Prematurely assessing the consequences of options can interfere with the creative process of generating them.

Questions and comments for generating and exploring options include: 'Given your goal of _____ [specify goal] what ways might you attain it?', 'Just let the ideas flow without editing them too much', 'Are there any other ways that you might approach the situation?' and 'What might be the consequences of doing that?' Notice that all of these questions and comments put the onus of coming up with ideas on the helpee. Resist the temptation to take over and own helpees' problem situations.

BOX 16.2   GENERATING OPTIONS TO ATTAIN GOALS: CASE EXAMPLE

THE PROBLEM SITUATION

Helen, 41, enters helping worried about her deteriorating relationships with her husband Oscar, 42, and daughter, Poppy, 14. Here her helper, Jack, 38, works with her on improving her relationship with Poppy. Helen admits to concentrating too much on her job and not spending much time as a mother with Poppy. Helen sees her as a bright girl who is at risk of getting out of control. Poppy does not seem to spend much time studying, sits around the house bored much of the time, and is starting to make some unruly friends. At times, Helen and Oscar argue in front of Poppy and she just leaves the room.

HELEN'S GOALS

1 To develop a better relationship with Poppy.
2 To help Poppy deal with the tasks of adolescence.

HELEN'S OPTIONS

With the assistance of Jack, the following are some of the options that Helen generates to attain her goals.

Goal 1: Options for developing a better relationship with Poppy

- Organizing my workload to ensure I have time for Oscar and Poppy.
- Greeting Poppy in a friendly way in the evening and when I get home from work.
- Telling Poppy that I want to improve my relationship with both her and Oscar.
- Never arguing with Oscar in front of Poppy.
- Taking an interest in what is going on in Poppy's life that she is prepared to share.
- Letting Poppy know that I would like to spend more time with her.
- Discussing with Poppy things that we might do together and as a family.
- Finding some things that we can do together.
- Committing myself to regularly doing things with Poppy.

Goal 2: Options for helping Poppy with the tasks of adolescence

- Behaving in such a way that Poppy knows I am available for her if and when she wants to talk.
- Taking an interest in Poppy's school-work.
- Taking an interest in Poppy's extra-curricular activities.
- Talking with Poppy about the facts of life in a non-threatening way.
- Letting Poppy know that I will help her to drive when she can take the driving test.
- Making sure that Poppy has a reasonable allowance.

When working with helpees, start by keeping matters simple. For instance, you might focus on exploring options to attain one goal and then only assist the helpee to generate a few options. If necessary, you should consider using either notepads or whiteboards. It is well nigh impossible for you and your helpees to keep in your heads the kind of detail I have illustrated in the above case example.

ASSISTING PLANNING

Once helpees have generated options, they need to choose those that they are prepared to implement. Plans can range from the simple to the detailed. Skills for facilitating planning include assisting helpees to choose options for attaining their goals, encouraging helpees to be specific about how they can implement the options and, where appropriate, sequencing them into a step-by-step plan with a time frame. When plans have been formulated, you can explore helpees' commitment to implementing them, including how to deal with any anticipated difficulties and setbacks. Furthermore, you can encourage them to write down plans to make them easier to remember. If they are returning for subsequent sessions or helping contacts, you can assist them in monitoring progress and in adjusting plans, if necessary. Box 16.3 illustrates a plan that Helen and her helper, Jack, formulate to meet her goal of developing a better relationship with her daughter Poppy.

BOX 16.3   EXAMPLE OF A PLAN

HELEN'S GOAL

To develop a better relationship with Poppy.

HELEN'S PLAN

Step 1   Starting today, every day greet Poppy in a friendly way in the morning and also when I get back from work, and take an interest in what is going on in Poppy's life that she is prepared to share. Furthermore, starting today, organize my workload to ensure I have time for Oscar and Poppy, and never argue with Oscar in front of Poppy.

Step 2   This weekend, let Poppy know that I want to improve my relationship with both her and Oscar, spend more time with her, and discuss and find things that we might do together.

Step 3   No later than one week after step 2, engage in at least one pleasant activity with Poppy.

Step 4   Thereafter, engage in at least one pleasant activity with Poppy at least every week. Ensure that some pleasant activities are done as a family.

Sometimes helpers and helpees either have or think that they have little time to develop plans. Take the example of a helper working with Mira, who after 16 years of marriage feels the pressing need to inform her husband

Ibrahim that she feels cool and insufficiently involved in their relationship, even though she respects him and most of the time their relationship is friendly. For some time Mira has been building up to this discussion with Ibrahim and wants to hold it this evening. Her helper asks her 'What do you want to achieve?' Mira replies that she wants to bring her feelings out in the open and see how Ibrahim responds. The helper then asks Mira 'What are skilful ways to handle the talk with Ibrahim?' and 'What are unskilful ways?' The helper then encourages Mira to be more specific about how she intends to handle her discussion with Ibrahim this evening.

Activity 16.1 Facilitating problem solving

1 Work with a partner who presents either a problem situation of her/his own or one based on a helpee seen elsewhere.
2 Conduct a helping session in which you build a collaborative relationship with the helpee. Together you and your helpee clarify the problem situation, and the session ends with a summary by you of the main ground covered so far.
3 Then you and your helpee adopt a facilitating problem-solving approach to change, including:

  • clarifying goals
  • generating and exploring options for attaining goals
  • developing a plan, and
  • exploring the helpee's commitment to, and anticipating difficulties in, implementing the plan.

4 After the session ends, hold a sharing and feedback discussion. It can be a good idea to record the session and play it back as part of the sharing and feedback.
5 If appropriate, reverse roles.

COACHING, DEMONSTRATING AND REHEARSING  17

CHAPTER GOALS

By studying and doing the activities in chis chapter you should:

- Understand the difference between helper-centred and helpee-centred coaching.
- Develop knowledge and skills about demonstrating.
- Develop skills for assisting helpees to rehearse.

When adopting the improving communications/actions and thoughts approach to change, helpers often find themselves in the position of using training skills to assist helpees to behave differently. Three important training skills are helpee-centred coaching, demonstrating and rehearsing.

HELPEE-CENTRED COACHING

When training helpees in improving how they communicate, act and think, it is important that you allow them to retain ownership of their problems and problem situations. Furthermore, you should strive to maintain a good collaborative relationship. The urge to teach and instruct can override respect for the helpees' potential to lead their own life and make the decisions that work best for them.

A useful distinction is that between helper-centred coaching and helpee-centred coaching. Helper-centred coaching essentially takes the jug and mug approach: helpers are the jugs pouring knowledge and skills into helpees' mugs. Helpers are in control and their comments take the form 'First you do this, then you do that, then you do that …' and so on. Helpees are passive *receptacles* who are allowed to assume little responsibility for the pace and direction of their learning. In reality, very few helpers would work as crudely as I have depicted.

Helpee-centred coaching respects helpees as autonomous human beings. Helpers, as helpee-centred coaches, develop plans to attain goals in conjunction with helpees and draw out and build upon helpees' existing knowledge and skills. Furthermore, they allow helpees to participate in decisions about the pace and direction of learning, and also assist them to improve their knowledge and skills in such ways that they can help themselves after ending helping.

Take the example of providing feedback about helpees' performances when rehearsing how to improve their verbal, vocal and body messages in a specific situation. Helper-centred coaches provide the feedback themselves as though they are the experts. Helpee-centred coaches try to develop the expertise of helpees by asking them to evaluate their own performances before providing feedback themselves. Even when they do provide feedback, helpee-centred coaches are prepared to discuss it and leave helpees with the final say regarding its validity for them.

DEMONSTRATING

Helpers can use demonstrations to assist helpees to develop different and better ways of communicating/acting and thinking. Furthermore, you can demonstrate how to accompany communicating or acting differently with appropriate self-talk. The following are some ways that you can demonstrate improved ways of behaving.

LIVE

Probably most helping demonstrations are live. You may use live demonstrations when initially presenting different ways of behaving and when coaching helpees afterwards. Live demonstrations have the advantage of here-and-now spontaneity. In addition, you can interact with helpees and modify their demonstrations as appropriate. Unless a recording is made, a limitation of live demonstration is that helpees have no copy to watch or listen to on their own. You can also encourage helpees to observe live demonstrations in their everyday lives. For instance, you can encourage shy people to observe and learn from the social skills of those more outgoing.

RECORDED

Especially if working with helpee populations who have similar problems, you can record your own video or audio demonstrations. When making recordings, you can erase and correct poor efforts until you get it right. In addition, you can use recordings made by other people, some of which are professionally made, for instance, relaxation recordings. Advantages of audio and video demonstrations are that they can be loaned to helpees and be listened to or viewed repeatedly.

VISUALIZED

You can ask helpees to visualize or imagine the demonstration scenes that you describe. They can be asked to visualize either themselves or someone else performing the targeted communications or actions. Visual demonstrations are only appropriate for helpees who can imagine scenes adequately. A potential drawback is that, even when instructions are given well, there may be important differences between what you describe and what helpees imagine. In general helpees visualize best when relaxed.

WRITTEN

Written demonstrations are more appropriate for assisting helpees to change how they think than to change how they communicate and act. However, written demonstrations that contain visual images, such as cartoon characters, can convey desirable communications and actions.

DEMONSTRATOR SKILLS

Helpers must know their material thoroughly to demonstrate competently. For example, if you have a sound grasp of assertiveness skills, you are more likely to demonstrate these skills adequately than if less sure of your ground. You need to pay attention to the characteristics of the demonstration. One issue is whether to demonstrate incorrect as well as correct behaviours. You may plan briefly to demonstrate negative behaviours as a way of highlighting positive ones. However, make sure not to confuse helpees and always have the major emphasis on correct rather than incorrect behaviours.

Take care how you introduce demonstrations. You may increase helpees' attention by telling them what to look out for and also informing them that afterwards you will ask them to perform what has been demonstrated. During and at the end of demonstrations you may ask helpees whether they understand the points shown. Furthermore, they can summarize the main points of demonstrations. Probably, the best way for you to check a helpee's learning is to observe and coach them as they perform demonstrated communications/actions and thoughts.

REHEARSING

Rehearsing is a possibly less threatening expression than role-playing. Some helpees become uncomfortable at the idea of role-playing. Feeling shy and vulnerable already, they think they will further expose themselves in role-plays. You may need to explain to helpees that rehearsing can assist them by allowing them to try out communicating differently in an environment where mistakes do not really matter. Rehearsing can provide knowledge and confidence for communicating effectively in actual problem situations.

One way to start rehearsing is to demonstrate targeted communications with or without the helpee playing the other person. For example, in Box 17.1, the helper Phil demonstrates Isla's communication goals with Isla role-playing her roommate, Lucy, who is being asked by her to discuss having some quiet time, before inviting Isla to rehearse being himself while Phil plays the part of the roommate.

Phil then coaches Isla through a number of rehearsals where she assertively asks her roommate to discuss having some quiet time.

BOX 17.1   EXAMPLE OF DEMONSTRATING, REHEARSING AND COACHING

Isla, 21, a psychology student coming up to her final exams, goes to see a helper, Phil. Isla is worried about doing well, since she has a place on a master's course, but it is conditional on her obtaining a good degree. Isla tells Phil about her problem with her roommate Lucy, 20, a history student who plays the radio loudly when she studies. On questioning Isla, Phil finds that, although Isla does not like studying with the noise, she has never really tried to stop it. With Phil's help, Isla develops the following assertive request to Lucy: 'I know you like to study with the radio on, but, until my final exams are over, I would appreciate it if, when the library closes and I have to study here, we can agree on some times when it is quiet.' Again with Phil's help, Isla decides that her vocal messages should be calm and firm, and her body messages should include making good eye contact and keeping a pleasant facial expression.

Phil then asks Isla to role-play Lucy playing the music loudly on the radio and then being asked by her (demonstrated by Phil) to have a discussion about quiet time. Isla role-plays Lucy, and Phil demonstrates the verbal, vocal and body messages about which they previously had agreed. Isla is happy with the way Phil asks, but says she will need to practise some follow-up responses to variations in how Lucy might behave. Phil tells her to concentrate on making her initial request well

(Continued)

(Continued)

to start with. They reverse roles and this time Isla rehearses playing herself. Her first request is insufficiently assertive. After asking Isla to evaluate herself, Phil coaches her, including demonstrating how he observed her verbal, vocal and body messages and how she could perform differently. With continued coaching by Phil, Isla rehearses her request a few times until she is reasonably confident that she can perform competently in the real situation. Then Phil rehearses Isla on how she might respond to different ways that Lucy might answer her request.

As in Box 17.1, helpers and helpees may need to generate and rehearse alternative scripts. You should train diversely rather than rigidly in order to provide them with the flexibility to communicate well across a range of contingencies. You can facilitate their contributions to the discussion prior to making your own suggestions. For instance, Phil could ask Isla 'What do you think are the main ways in which Lucy might respond to your assertive request for a discussion about quiet time?' Afterwards, for each of the main ways identified, Phil could ask 'What verbal, vocal and bodily messages do you need to use to respond effectively?' Then, Isla and Phil could rehearse effective communications for different ways that Lucy might respond.

Process each rehearsal. You can ask helpees questions like: 'How do you think you did?', 'How were you feeling in that rehearsal?', and 'What difficulties might you face in communicating like that in the real situation?' In addition, you can provide both feedback and encouragement. Sometimes, you can audio record or visually record rehearsals and use the playback for feedback and discussion.

Activity 17.1   Using demonstrating skills

Work with a partner, with one of you taking the role of helper and the other taking the role of helpee. Helpee and helper hold a discussion to choose a specific communication that the helpee wants to improve. Do not attempt too much. The helper then goes through the following steps in a demonstration:

- cueing the helpee what to observe
- demonstrating each of the verbal, vocal and body message components of the communication
- then putting all three together (your partner may role-play the other person as you demonstrate)
- asking the helpee to summarize the main points of the demonstration.

Afterwards hold a sharing and discussion session focused on the helper's use of demonstration skills. If necessary repeat the demonstration until the helper feels s/he has obtained some degree of competence in using demonstration skills.

Then reverse roles.

Activity 17.2   Using rehearsing and coaching skills

Work with a partner, with one of you taking the role of helper and the other taking the role of helpee. Either for a specific communication that was demonstrated in Activity 17.1 or for another specific communication that the helpee wants to improve, go through the following sequence:

- cueing the helpee what to observe
- demonstrating each of the verbal, vocal and body message components of the communication and then putting all three together (your partner may role-play the other person as you demonstrate)
- asking the helpee to summarize the main points of the demonstration
- introducing the idea of rehearsing the communication to your helpee
- rehearsing and coaching your helpee to the point where, within the limits of this activity, s/he feels competent to perform the communication in real life. You may use audio or video playback as part of the rehearsing and coaching process.

Afterwards hold a sharing and discussion session focused on the helper's use of rehearsing and coaching skills. If necessary, allow the helper to rehearse and coach some more until the helper feels s/he has obtained some degree of competence in using rehearsing and coaching skills.

Then reverse roles.

IMPROVING HELPEES' SELF-TALK

18

CHAPTER GOALS

By studying and doing the activity in this chapter you should:

- Know about calming, coaching and affirming self-talk.
- Be able to assist helpees to make composite self-talk statements.

The next three chapters focus on working with how helpees think. I present the three central mind skills of creating self-talk, rules and perceptions in an introductory way to provide a basic toolkit for helpers to assist helpees in improving their thinking. Each of the chosen mind skills has wide applicability.

Proceed with great caution when assisting helpees to alter specific thoughts. I have witnessed some beginning helpers jump in with faulty analyses of thinking, which helpees have not had the knowledge or confidence to challenge. In addition, if you do not understand the mind skills properly yourself, you will present them in a confused way. Furthermore, sometimes helpers rush through learning sequences rather than training them thoroughly.

Those of you with reasonable skills at working with your own thinking will probably have more insight into how to work with helpees' thinking than those with poor mind skills. A good way to learn about how to use mind skills is to become proficient at using them in your own life.

At first, it is probably easiest to focus on working with one mind skill, before broadening your repertoire. Creating self-talk is a good mind skills area with which to start. One reason for this is that helpees can create self-talk that supports any changed communication or action they target. Another reason is that virtually all helpers and helpees are aware that they talk to themselves anyway. So requesting that they do so in a more disciplined way is unlikely to be too strange.

You can use visual aids when working with helpees' thinking. I find using a whiteboard can be helpful, especially when it comes to collaborating to generate and refine more effective thoughts. I have seen some prominent psychotherapists use notepads. At an appropriate moment, you should encourage helpees to make their own visual records by writing their improved thoughts down.

Helpees have usually built up and sustained their ways of faulty thinking over many years and, consequently, quick fixes are unlikely to succeed. You can protect them if you keep offering a good collaborative relationship. In addition to using good active listening skills, you can coach them in improving their thinking in helpee-centred rather than helper-centred ways. Humility is in order and, at all costs, you should avoid being an instant and overbearing expert.

IMPROVING SELF-TALK

I encourage you to try the simple mind experiment of closing your eyes for 30 seconds and trying to think of nothing. Most of you will become very aware that you cannot rid yourself of self-talk.

NEGATIVE SELF-TALK

People who talk to themselves are not crazy. It is what they choose to keep telling themselves that determines sanity or insanity. Here, self-talk refers to talking to yourself before, during and after difficult situations. Often helpees use negative self-talk that has the effect of creating or worsening self-defeating feelings, physical reactions and actions. Characteristics of negative self-talk include self-disparagement, stating that matters may get either worse or out of control, and focusing on past setbacks. Box 18.1 provides an illustration of a helpee who interferes with her effectiveness by using negative self-talk.

BOX 18.1   EXAMPLE OF NEGATIVE SELF-TALK

Olivia, 25, is a shy single woman who gets very anxious about going to parties. Before she goes to a party, she tenses up and tells herself statements like 'I always find parties difficult and never succeed at getting relaxed' and 'I'm going to have another difficult experience.' When Olivia is at a party she says to herself 'I wonder what they are thinking of me', 'My social skills are poor', and 'I'm feeling anxious and wonder if my anxiety is going to get out of control'. After a party she tells herself 'I'm glad that it is over, since I failed to relax again' and 'I'm never going to enjoy myself at parties.'

COPING SELF-TALK

Coping self-talk contrasts with negative self-talk. Whereas negative self-talk impedes helpees from communicating and acting appropriately, coping self-talk enhances the likelihood of their performing well. Coping self-talk can be contrasted with mastery self-talk. Coping self-talk is about doing as well as you reasonably can rather than seeking the unrealistically high standards of mastery or perfection. The following are three key dimensions of coping self-talk.

CALMING SELF-TALK

Creating calming self-talk can assist helpees to deal with problem situations in many ways. Before, during and after specific situations, they can calm their minds so that they can better handle unwanted feelings such as harmful anxiety or excessive anger. In addition, they may wish to calm and relax their mind as a way of managing extraneous stresses that then impact on how they handle problem situations. A third purpose for creating calming self-talk is to become more centred and focused when wishing to think through, or talk through, how best to communicate or act in problem situations. Helpees' use of calming self-talk helps them to clear a psychological space for getting in touch with their feelings and thinking more sharply and deeply.

When introducing calming self-talk, I may talk about the concept and then provide an example of a calming self-instruction like 'Relax'. I encourage helpees to come up with some calming self-instructions of their own. Then we may discuss which calming self-instructions they prefer to use. In addition, I tell, demonstrate and coach them in how to use a calm and measured voice when giving calming self-instructions. Sometimes, I highlight the difference by saying a phrase like 'Calm down' in a hurried and self-pressurizing way.

Cooling self-talk statements might be regarded as a sub-category of calming self-talk. You can train helpees who are prone to angry outbursts with cooling self-talk statements. Box 18.2 provides examples of both calming and cooling self-talk statements.

BOX 18.2   EXAMPLES OF CALMING AND COOLING SELF-TALK STATEMENTS

CALMING SELF-TALK STATEMENTS

Keep calm

Slow down

Relax

Take it easy

Take a deep breath

Breathe slowly and regularly

I can manage

COOLING SELF-TALK STATEMENTS

Cool it

Count to ten

Be careful

Don't overreact

Don't let my pride get in the way

I can choose not to let myself get hooked

Problem-solve

COACHING SELF-TALK

Coaching self-talk is no substitute for possessing the communication skills for achieving a task. The first step in coaching self-talk is to assist helpees to break tasks down. You can work with them to think through systematic approaches to attaining goals in problem situations, including how to handle setbacks. Once plans are clear, helpees then require the ability to instruct themselves through the steps of implementing them.

Emphasize self-talk about vocal and body as well as verbal messages. Take the example of Isla, the psychology student in Box 17.1, who together with her helper Phil developed the assertive verbal message to her room-mate, Lucy, 'I know you like to study with the radio on, but, until my final exams are over, I would appreciate it if, when the library closes and I have to study here, we can agree on some times when it is quiet.' As well as coaching Isla in how to handle the face-to-face interaction, Phil could train her to rehearse in her mind giving herself appropriate self-instructions about her verbal, vocal and body messages. Isla's targeted vocal messages were to be calm and firm, and her targeted body messages were to make good eye contact and to keep a pleasant facial expression. When on her own, Isla could then use visualized rehearsal to coach herself in coping better in the situation. You can also assist clients to develop coaching self-talk statements to handle different ways other people in problem situations might respond.

AFFIRMING SELF-TALK

I prefer the notion of affirming self-talk to that of positive self-talk. The danger of positive self-talk is that helpees may tell themselves false positives that set them up for disappointment and failure. Affirming self-talk focuses on reminding yourself of realistic factors that count in your favour. What follows are some aspects of affirming self-talk.

First, helpees can tell themselves that they can cope. Sample self-statements include: 'I can handle this situation', 'My anxiety is a signal for me to use my coping skills', and 'All I have to do is to cope'. In addition, once they cope with situations better, they can acknowledge this, for example, 'I used my coping skills and they worked.'

Second, helpees can acknowledge their strengths. Often when anxious about difficult situations, they forget their strengths. For example, when asking for dates, they may genuinely possess good points, so they do not have to boast about them. Also, they may have good conversational skills that they can acknowledge and use rather than thinking about what may go wrong. In addition, they can think about any successful experiences they may have had in past situations similar to the one they now face.

Third, helpees may become more confident if they acknowledge supportive people to whom they have access. For instance, relatives, friends, spouses and helping-service professionals might each be sources of support, though not necessarily so. Just realizing they have supportive people to whom they can turn may be sufficient to help some cope better with problem situations.

PUTTING IT ALL TOGETHER

Often calming, coaching and affirming self-talk statements are combined together. Box 18.3 continues the example of going-to-party anxious Isla from Box 17.1 to show how her helper Phil assisted her to have the option of telling herself a composite calming, coaching and affirming coping-self-talk statement. At the end of the session, Isla writes down her coping self-talk statements for remembering, rehearsing and using outside of helping.

BOX 18.3   EXAMPLE OF COPING SELF-TALK

Isla's helper, Phil, first put the word calming on the whiteboard and then helped her to identify statements she would find useful to calm herself down when thinking of a party in advance. Phil and Isla repeated this process for coaching,

---

affirming and composite statements. They ended with the following categories and statements written on the whiteboard.

CALMING

Take it easy

Relax

COACHING

Remember to talk as well as to listen

Spend time with people I like

When listening, show that I have understood

I can retrieve mistakes

AFFIRMING

I'm getting better at this

Well done. I know I can do it

COMPOSITE

Take it easy. Remember to talk as well as to listen. I'm getting better at this.

Activity 18.1   Assisting a helpee to use coping self-talk

Work with a partner who either uses a personal concern or role-plays a helpee, with a goal of using coping self-talk to manage a problem situation better. Within the context of a good collaborative relationship and, possibly, using a whiteboard during the process:

- use speaking skills to describe the difference between negative and coping self-talk
- use demonstrating skills
- assist the helpee to identify any current negative self-talk
- use coaching skills to assist the helpee to formulate calming, coaching and affirming self-talk statements
- use negotiating homework skills.

Afterwards discuss and reverse roles. Playing back audio or video recordings of rehearsal and practice sessions may assist learning.

IMPROVING HELPEES' RULES

19

CHAPTER GOALS

By studying and doing the activity in this chapter you should:

- Know about detecting demanding rules.
- Be able to assist helpees to dispute demanding rules.
- Enable helpees to state preferential rules.

Helpers can assist helpees to replace their demanding rules with ones that are more realistic. All people possess rule books that provide us with ready-made guidelines for leading our lives so that we do not need to think through all emerging situations from scratch. Most of the rules of well-functioning people are rational, realistic and based on our preferences for ourselves, others and the environment. However, many helpees contribute to disturbing themselves and making themselves unhappy because, often unawares, they possess some significant rigid or demanding rules, based on making irrational and unrealistic demands on themselves, others and the environment.

DETECTING DEMANDING RULES

Unrealistic and demanding rules significantly contribute to many helpees having difficulty managing their problems and problem situations. Demanding rules can lay the foundation for creating negative self-talk and inaccurate perceptions. For example, demanding rules like 'I must get approval' and 'I must be perfect' probably underlie many people's feelings of lack of confidence and well-being before starting new tasks, like writing essays. You can rationally prefer that readers like your essays and that you write them competently. These preferences are very different from essay writers demanding approval from readers and perfection from themselves.

Usually, demanding rules contain realistic as well as unrealistic parts. For example, it is realistic for essay writers to want to write competently, but unrealistic to strive for perfection. Consequently, when assisting helpees to alter a rule, focus on discarding the 20 to 30 per cent of the rule that is irrational, rather than getting rid of it altogether.

The following are some indicators or signals to look out for when trying to detect demanding rules. You can pay attention to signs of inappropriate language. For example, demanding rules tend to be characterized by 'musts', 'oughts', 'shoulds' and 'have tos'. The following are four of the main demanding or, to use Albert Ellis's term, 'mustabatory' rules:

- I must be liked by everyone
- I must be perfectly competent
- Other people must do what I want
- Life must be fair.

Persistent inappropriate feelings can signal that helpees possess a demanding rule. The dividing line between appropriate and inappropriate feelings is not always clear. Life can be difficult, so appropriate feelings cannot simply be equated with 'positive' feelings like happiness, joy and accomplishment. Some 'negative' feelings like sadness, grief, fear and anger can be entirely appropriate for the contexts in which they occur. You have to ask yourself questions like: 'Is this feeling appropriate for the situation?' and 'Is keeping feeling this way helping or harming the helpee?' Physical reactions may also signal demanding rules, for instance, persistent muscular tension could signal helpees putting pressure on themselves for perfection or universal approval.

Inappropriate feelings, physical reactions and communications/ actions are interrelated. If helpees feel excessively angry because of a demanding rule, their physical level of arousal can impair their judgment to the point where they act violently and worsen rather than help their position. Relevant questions to ask yourself, and possibly helpees too, include: 'Are helpees' communications or actions helping or harming themselves or others?', 'Are they overreacting?', and 'Is their behaviour self-defeating?'

Box 19.1 provides an illustration of the consequences of workaholic student Jacob's demanding rule 'I must get a very good degree' in regard to his upcoming final exams. I have presented this example in the STC (Situation–Thoughts–Consequences) format that I first introduced in Chapter 12 when reviewing monitoring. Since this example has a second part in Box 19.3, I have indicated Jacob's present thoughts and their consequences by putting (1) after T and C.

BOX 19.1   EXAMPLE OF A DEMANDING RULE AND ITS CONSEQUENCES

S   Workaholic student Jacob has final exams coming up and is becoming increasingly anxious.

T (1)   *Demanding rule*: 'I must get a very good degree.'

C (1)   *Negative feelings consequences* include anxiety, feeling very stressed, irritability and low self-esteem.

Negative physical reaction consequences include mental tension, difficulty sleeping and exhaustion.

    Negative communication/action consequences include spending excessive time revising – not always very productively – giving up all social life and taking inadequate recreation.

How can you assist helpees to create preferential rules to replace their demanding rules? Reading the signals, you can assist them to identify what might be one or more underlying demanding rules relevant to their problem situations. Then you can encourage them to dispute, question and challenge their demanding rules and to restate them as preferential rules.

DISPUTING DEMANDING RULES

Albert Ellis considered disputing to be the most typical and often-used method of his Rational Emotive Behaviour Therapy. Disputing means challenging demanding rules. The main skill in challenging is that of scientific questioning. You and your helpees can use reason, logic and facts to support, discard or amend any rule considered to be potentially demanding. Box 19.2 shows two methods of disputing demanding rules.

BOX 19.2   TWO METHODS OF DISPUTING DEMANDING RULES

FUNCTIONAL DISPUTING

Functional disputing aims to point out to helpees that their rules may be interfering with them attaining their goals. Typical questions are:

- Is it helping you?
- How is continuing to think this way (or behave, or feel this way) affecting your life?

EMPIRICAL DISPUTING

Empirical disputing aims to help helpees evaluate the factual components of their rules. Typical questions are:

- Where is the evidence that you must succeed at all important tasks you prefer?
- Where is the proof that it is accurate?
- Where is it written?

When collaborating with helpees to dispute demanding rules, elicit some questions from them, for instance, 'How might you question or challenge that rule?' When asking questions, do so gently rather than forcefully, and respond to helpees' answers the same way. Furthermore, show restraint in the amount of questions you ask, and remember to integrate active listening into the questioning and disputing process.

STATING PREFERENTIAL RULES

Assisting helpees to dispute their demanding rules should have the effect of loosening their effect on them. An added way of reducing the hold of demanding rules is to assist helpees to restate them succinctly into preferential rules. Their challenges can be too many and varied to remember easily. Helpers can assist clients to create replacement statements that are easy to remember and recall. Sometimes, when time is very limited, you may eliminate time spent on questioning and challenging, and move straight into helping them to restate a demanding rule as a preferential rule.

You and your helpees can alter characteristics of demanding rules to become characteristics of preferential rules. An example is 'I'd PREFER to do very well but I don't HAVE TO'. Helpees can replace rules about mastery and perfection with rules incorporating competence, coping and 'doing as well as I can under the circumstances'. Furthermore, you can assist them to refrain from rating their whole selves rather than evaluating how useful their specific communications and actions are.

In addition, you can assist helpees to avoid making out that the world is absolutely awful by accepting that the world is imperfect and by refraining from exaggerating negative factors and possibilities. You can also help them to eliminate an 'I-can't-stand-it' attitude by encouraging them to tell themselves that they can stand the anxiety and discomfort arising from themselves, others and the environment not being as they would prefer them to be. Indeed, even in genuinely adverse circumstances, they may have many strengths on which they can rely and supportive persons to whom they can turn.

When working on restating rules, encourage helpees to participate in the process by sharing their ideas. Some helpers use a whiteboard and work together with helpees to get the wording just right for them to recall and use in future. The following are examples of how to restate four common demanding rules into preferential rules.

Demanding rule: I must be liked by everyone.

Preferential rule: I would prefer to have most people like me, but what is really important is that some significant people whom I respect like me and that I approve of myself.

Demanding rule: I must be perfectly competent.

Preferential rule: I prefer to strive towards high standards, but all I can do is the best I can.

Demanding rule: Other people must do what I want.

Preferential rule: I would prefer that others take my wishes into account, but I need to be sensitive to their wishes too.

Demanding rule: Life must be fair.

Preferential rule: I would prefer that life be fair, but the world is imperfect and I accept that there may be some aspects of it I cannot change.

Encourage helpees to work and practise hard to maintain their preferential rules. One approach is to make recordings of helpees' initial demanding rules, their challenges and their restatements. They can also post in prominent positions reminder cards stating their preferential rules. In addition, they can use visualized rehearsals in which they imagine themselves in a specific situation experiencing the negative consequences arising from their demanding rule. Then they can imagine switching over to their preferential rule and visualize the positive consequences of doing so. Last, but not least, assist and encourage helpees to change how they communicate and act in line with their improved rules. Box 19.3 shows the revised consequences C (2) for exam-anxious Jacob for successfully adhering to his improved preferential rule T (2).

**BOX 19.3   EXAMPLE OF A PREFERENTIAL RULE
AND ITS CONSEQUENCES**

S   Workaholic student Jacob has final exams coming up and is becoming increasingly anxious.

T (1)   *Demanding rule*:'I must get a very good degree.'

T (2) *Preferential rule* 'I prefer to get a very good degree but all I can do is revise sensibly, keep reasonably fresh, and answer the exam questions carefully.'

C (2) *Positive feelings consequences* include less anxiety and greater happiness.

Positive physical reactions consequences include sleeping better and being less mentally tense and exhausted.

Positive action consequences include spending slightly less time revising (yet being more productive), having some social life and enjoying some recreation.

Activity 19.1 Assisting a helpee to improve a rule

Work with a partner who either uses a personal concern or role-plays a helpee, with a mind goal of creating one or more preferential rules to manage a problem situation better. Within the context of a good collaborative relationship and, possibly, using a whiteboard during the process:

- use speaking skills to describe the difference between demanding and preferential rules;
- use demonstrating skills;
- cooperate with the helpee to identify any major demanding rules and put the main one into the STC framework;
- use coaching skills to assist the helpee to question and challenge the main demanding rule;
- use coaching skills to assist the helpee to create a preferential rule statement to replace the demanding rule;
- together with the helpee anticipate the consequences of her/him managing to maintain using her/his preferential rule; and
- use negotiating homework skills.

Afterwards discuss and reverse roles. Playing back audio recordings or video recordings of rehearsal and practice sessions may assist learning.

IMPROVING HELPEES' PERCEPTIONS

CHAPTER GOALS

By studying and doing the activity in this chapter you should:

- Be able to assist helpees to elicit and identify automatic perceptions.
- Get helpees to check the accuracy of their perceptions.
- Enable helpees to choose the best fit perception(s).

A Chinese proverb states 'Two-thirds of what we see is behind our eyes'. Helpees may have systematic biases in how they interpret information. Often these biases work against their happiness and fulfilment. Closely observe how much evidence they provide to support assertions about how they and others behave.

PERCEIVING AND INTERPRETING

When training helpees to improve their skills at creating perceptions, helpers can start by teaching them the importance of examining the connections between how they think, feel and act. You can introduce the concept of automatic thoughts or perceptions and provide an example of how underlying perceptions can influence feelings. The American psychiatrist Aaron Beck uses the example of instructing a male helpee to imagine a person was at home one night who hears a crash in another room. When asked how the person might react to the first interpretation, 'There's a burglar in the room', the helpee replied that he would feel 'very anxious, terrified' and that he might hide or phone the police. The helpee thought the person would react to the second interpretation 'The windows have been left open and the wind has caused something to fall over', by not being afraid, but possibly being sad if something valuable had broken. The person would probably go to see what the problem was. Beck explained to him that this example illustrates that there are a number of ways that people can interpret situations and that the way they interpret situations affects how they feel and behave.

Related to showing the influence of perceptions on feelings and behaviour, you can also train helpees to understand the difference between fact and inference. They can learn that their perceptions of themselves, others and the world are their subjective 'facts'. Often, however, they may fail to realize that these perceptions may be based on inference rather than fact. A favourite illustration of this point by one of my Stanford University professors was: 'All Indians walk in single file … at least the one I saw did.' That one Indian was seen is a fact; that they all walk in single file is an inference.

Helpees can make inferences about themselves, others and the environment. They can be both positive and negative. They are of varying degrees of accuracy concerning the factual data on which they are based. Box 20.1 provides two examples of the difference between fact and inference.

BOX 20.1   EXAMPLES OF THE DIFFERENCE BETWEEN FACT AND INFERENCE

EXAMPLE 1

Fact: I lose my job when the company is forced to cut staff by 20 per cent overall and, especially, in my department.

Inference: I was not doing a good job.

EXAMPLE 2

Fact: My partner is unusually irritable with me.

Inference: She/he is losing interest in me.

Note: In each of the above examples the facts and evidence did not justify the inferences.

I stress the distinction between fact and inference because it is a theme that underlies how helpees create and persist in creating inaccurate perceptions. They may both jump to conclusions and also remain unaware that they have taken the leap. Illusion then becomes their reality, in whole or in part.

ELICITING AND IDENTIFYING AUTOMATIC PERCEPTIONS

In order to change their thinking, helpees first need to become aware of their automatic perceptions. The following are some salient characteristics of such perceptions. Automatic perceptions:

- are part of people's internal monologue – what and how they talk to themselves;
- can take the form of words, images or both;
- occur very rapidly and usually at the fringe of awareness;
- can precede and accompany emotions, including feelings and inhibitions – for instance, people's emotional responses to each other's actions follow from their inter-pretations rather than from the actions themselves;
- are generally plausible to people who assume that they are accurate; and
- have a recurring quality, despite people trying to block them out.

Though often hard to identify, you can train helpees to pinpoint possibly inaccurate automatic perceptions. You may question them about automatic perceptions that occur during upsetting situations. Where they experience difficulty in recalling thoughts, you may use either imagery or role-playing. When questioning, observe carefully for signs of emotion that may offer leads for further questioning. The use of a whiteboard can help. When helpees see their initial thoughts written up on the board, this may trigger them to reveal less obvious and more frightening thoughts.

Helpees may be set homework assignments in which they record their thoughts and perceptions. They can complete daily worksheets in which they record, in their separate columns:

- *Situation(s)* leading to negative emotion(s)
- *Feelings and physical reaction(s)* felt and their degree on a 0–100 scale
- *Automatic perceptions and image(s)* and a rating of how strongly they believed the automatic perception(s) on a 0–100 scale. In addition, they can identify any particu-larly hot perceptions.

You can also request that helpees fill in worksheets identifying and rating key feelings, physical reactions, perceptions and images for specific prob-lem situations they encounter between sessions (see Box 12.1). Again, they can be asked to identify hot perceptions.

CHECKING THE ACCURACY OF PERCEPTIONS

When faced with problem situations, helpees may make potentially errone-ous statements about themselves, such as 'I'm no good at that', and about others, such as 'She/he always does ...' or 'She/he never does ...'. Such state-ments or perceptions influence how they feel and communicate and act. When assisting them to check the accuracy of their perceptions, you are asking them to distinguish between fact and inference, and to make their inferences fit the facts as closely as possible.

Encourage helpees to think of their perceptions as propositions that together you can investigate to see how far they are supported by evidence. An example provided by Aaron Beck is that of a resident who insisted that 'I am not a good doctor'. Therapist and helpee listed criteria for being a good doctor. The resident then monitored his behaviour and sought feedback from supervisors and colleagues. Finally, he concluded: 'I am a good doctor after all'.

As shown in Box 20.2, you can assist helpees to check the accuracy of their perceptions in problem situations by asking three main questions:

- Where is the evidence for your perception?
- Are there any other ways of perceiving the situation?
- Which way(s) of perceiving the situation best fit(s) the available facts?

BOX 20.2   EXAMPLE OF CHECKING THE ACCURACY OF A PERCEPTION

PROBLEM SITUATION

Six months ago Aloka, 26, started her first teaching job at a large inner-city secondary school. Roger, 44, who became headmaster a year ago and is determined to raise the school's quality, hired Aloka. Roger likes to keep in touch with the staff and encourages them to let him know how they are getting on. Aloka goes to Roger and tells him that she is finding the job very difficult and wonders whether she has the skills and the stamina to succeed. Roger listens at first and then, during the course of their conversation, asks Aloka the following three questions.

ALOKA'S POTENTIALLY ERRONEOUS PERCEPTION

'I am not succeeding as a teacher in this school.'

QUESTION 1: 'WHERE IS THE EVIDENCE FOR YOUR PERCEPTION?'

When asked this question Aloka talks about how she finds it difficult to keep order in class. She finds the pupils very talkative, much more talkative than at the schools where she trained. Aloka says that she would like to keep more order. However, she admits that, on the whole, the pupils' work is improving and that they are quite friendly to her.

QUESTION 2: 'ARE THERE ANY OTHER WAYS OF PERCEIVING THE SITUATION?'

'The pupils would do better if they had another teacher.'

'The pupils are too bad to be helped properly.'

(Continued)

(Continued)

'The previous teacher was far too permissive and the pupils did what they liked too much.'

'I need to work on my class control skills.'

'The pupils are starting to chat less and focus on work more.'

'I need to get some support and advice on how to improve my teaching skills.'

'I spend too much time worrying and not enough enjoying myself.'

QUESTION 3 'WHICH WAY(S) OF PERCEIVING THE SITUATION BEST FIT(S) THE AVAILABLE FACTS?'

After some thought, Aloka decides that the most accurate perceptions are:

'The pupils are starting to chat less and focus on work more.'

'I need to work on my class control skills.'

'I need to get some support and advice on how to improve my teaching skills.'

Insufficient confidence can be a big problem when taking on a difficult job. In the example in Box 20.2, Aloka is fortunate enough to have a headmaster, Roger, who in the context of a good collaborative relationship, helps her to gain insight into a potentially dangerous automatic perception. Had Aloka persisted in her automatic perception, which left her feeling a failure and not knowing what to do, she might well have resigned from her job. The result of Aloka thinking more deeply about her automatic perception was that she calmed down and managed to see her teaching duties in perspective, including that she could improve.

You can go beyond assisting helpees to change single inaccurate automatic perceptions, to make them more aware that they may have a tendency to process information in biased ways. For instance, in future, when faced with similar feelings of lack of confidence, Aloka could use the skills of questioning herself to test the reality of her perceptions. You may also assist clients to alter thoughts in more than one mind skills area. For instance, you might encourage Aloka to challenge and alter a demanding rule such as 'I must be the perfect teacher.' Furthermore, Aloka could learn to use calming and coaching self-talk to guide her in communicating assertively rather than submissively with the pupils.

Activity 20.1 Assisting a helpee to test the reality of a perception

Work with a partner who either uses a personal concern or role-plays a helpee, with a goal of creating one or more realistic perceptions to manage a problem situation better. Within the context of a good collaborative relationship and, possibly, using a whiteboard during the process:

- Use speaking skills to describe the importance of reality-testing perceptions rather than jumping to conclusions.
- Use demonstrating skills.
- Cooperate with the helpee to identify a possibly inaccurate automatic perception concerning the situation.
- Assist your helpee to test the reality of the automatic perception by asking her/him the questions:

  o 'Where is the evidence for your perception?'
  o 'Are there any other ways of perceiving the situation?'
  o 'Which way(s) of perceiving the situation best fit(s) the available facts?'

- Use negotiating homework skills.

Afterwards, discuss and reverse roles. Playing back audio or video recordings of rehearsal and practice sessions may assist learning.

NEGOTIATING HOMEWORK

CHAPTER GOALS

By studying and doing the activities in this chapter you should:

- Know about different formats for homework.
- Be able to increase helpees' compliance with homework assignments.
- Start identifying supports and resources for helpees to use.

The theme of this chapter is that of how, during helping, helpees can use the time in between contacts with their helpers to best effect. On many occasions you may find it useful to discuss homework activities that they might undertake before you meet again. In formal counselling these would be between-session activities. Here I use the term negotiating homework, because of the large variety of settings and ways in which helping takes place. In some settings the word 'homework' might be considered stuffy or inappropriate because of its educational connotations. If so, use the terminology that works best for you. For the sake of simplicity, much of the following discussion on negotiating homework assumes formal helping sessions. Consequently, if this assumption is inaccurate, adapt the discussion to your special circumstances.

NEGOTIATING HOMEWORK

After presenting, demonstrating and coaching helpees in improved ways of thinking and communicating/acting, in the context of collaborative relationships you can negotiate relevant homework assignments. Homework assignments include trying out changed behaviours in real life and filling out self-monitoring sheets and worksheets for developing mind skills that influence feelings, communications and actions. Other assignments can entail reading self-help books, listening to and watching audio or video recordings, and observing people with good communication skills.

Many reasons exist for suggesting homework assignments. These reasons include speeding up the learning process and encouraging helpees to monitor, rehearse and practise changed communications and actions. Furthermore, homework activities can help the transfer of behaviours worked on in helping to real life. Sometimes, when this happens, helpees experience difficulties in applying their improved behaviours. Such difficulties may be addressed when you next meet. In addition, homework assignments can increase their sense of self-control and of personal responsibility for improving how they think, communicate and act.

One of the central problems in assigning homework activities is getting helpees to do them. Often as a counsellor trainer I have observed trainees rush through negotiating homework assignments at the end of sessions in ways that virtually guaranteed non-compliance. Common mistakes included not leaving enough time, inviting insufficient helpee participation, giving vague verbal instructions, and not checking whether helpees clearly understood what they were meant to do. Box 21.1 lists nine guidelines recommended by prominent American cognitive therapists Christine Padesky and Dennis Greenberger for increasing the chances of compliance.

BOX 21.1   GUIDELINES FOR INCREASING COMPLIANCE WITH HOMEWORK ASSIGNMENTS

1 Make assignments small.
2 Assign tasks within the helpee's skill level.
3 Make assignments relevant and interesting.
4 Collaborate with the helpee in developing learning assignments.
5 Provide a clear rationale for the assignment and a written summary.
6 Begin the assignment during the session.
7 Identify and problem-solve impediments to the assignment.
8 Emphasize learning, not a desired outcome.
9 Show interest, and follow up in the next appointment.

You can design your own homework assignment forms or write down tailor-made instructions as occasions arise. These may be either the best or only options for informal helping contexts. Box 21.2 presents four formats for homework forms based on the assumption of formal helping sessions. Where possible, either you or your helpee should write down clear instructions for homework assignments on these forms. Writing instructions on scraps of paper is generally not good enough. Always check what helpees write, to make sure they have taken down the instructions correctly. If you want them to fill out forms such as monitoring logs, provide these forms yourself. This practice ensures clear instructions and saves helpees the extra effort of having to write out forms before filling them in.

BOX 21.2   FORMATS FOR HOMEWORK FORMS

FORMAT 1

Homework assignment form

In order to gain the most from your helping session(s) you are encouraged to engage in the following between-session activities.

FORMAT 2

To follow up

In order to gain the most from your helping session(s) you are encouraged to perform the following tasks.

FORMAT 3

Take-away sheet

Use this sheet for writing down (1) your main learnings from helping and (2) any instructions for between-session activities.

FORMAT 4

Learning contract

I make a learning contract with myself to perform the following activities before the next helping session.

Note: As appropriate, substitute the word 'counselling' for 'helping'.

Sometimes, changing a way of communicating or acting requires helpees to give up long-established habits. Here it can be especially important not to agree on too difficult an activity too soon. Where possible try to build in some early successes to encourage persistence in working on skills.

Some helpees return to non-supportive, if not downright hostile, environments. In such cases you may need to prepare them more thoroughly prior to suggesting they implement their improved communications and actions outside of helping. Such preparation may include devising strategies for coping with negative feedback.

Last, signal a joint progress review by letting helpees know that, when you next meet, you will ask them how they fared in their homework assignments. Helpees who know that you are interested in and supportive of their attempts to complete homework assignments are more likely to be motivated to do so, that is, so long as you avoid becoming controlling and judgmental.

IDENTIFYING SUPPORTS AND RESOURCES

The need to identify supports and resources outside of helping overlaps with that of negotiating homework. Both focus on assisting helpees to use time well outside of helping. You may need to raise their awareness about the importance of identifying and using supports and of lessening contact with non-supportive people. You can assist them to identify people in their home environments who can support their efforts to improve how they think, communicate and act. For example, a helpee with a drinking problem might be encouraged to join Alcoholics Anonymous. Another example is helping university students with poor study skills to seek out sympathetic lecturers and tutors to assist them, for instance in writing more polished essays or revising well for examinations. Unemployed people can approach friends and relatives who may not only offer them emotional support, but also be sources for job leads. Women working on verbal, vocal and body messages for communicating more assertively can seek out women's groups where they may find other women with similar objectives.

An inverse approach to support is to assist helpees in identifying unsympathetic or counterproductive people. They are then left with various choices: getting such people to accept, if not support, their efforts to change; seeing less of them; or stopping seeing them altogether. If these people are family members, avoiding them altogether may be difficult, especially if helpees are financially dependent on them. Here, you may discuss damage control strategies. However, helpees can often choose their friendship and membership groups and therefore may be able to change the company they keep.

You can enlist a variety of people as aides such as partners, teachers, parents, welfare workers, supervisors and friends. Some guidelines for using third parties as helper's aides include obtaining the permission of helpees, identifying suitable people and, where necessary, training them in their roles. An example of using third parties as aides is that of asking teachers to help shy and lonely pupils to participate more in class.

In addition, you can assist helpees to identify and use resources for helping them attain and maintain improved ways of thinking, communicating and acting. Such resources include workshops and short courses, self-help books and manuals, instructional audio or video recordings, appropriate voluntary agencies, peer support groups and networks, telephone hotlines, and crisis information outlets.

Become familiar with and, possibly, establish contact with the human supports and educational and information resources of most relevance to the populations with which you work. Access to suitable supports and resources may be of tremendous assistance to some helpees as they take positive steps towards changing how they think, communicate and act in problem areas.

Activity 21.1   Negotiating homework

Work with a partner who selects a problem situation in which she/he wants to communicate better. Collaborate with your partner to identify some key verbal, vocal and body messages in need of improvement. Using coaching, demonstrating and rehearsing, assist your partner to improve her/his skills. Then rehearse and practise how to negotiate one or more homework activities so that your partner can use the time (assume a week) before you next meet to good effect. To increase chances of compliance, observe the following guidelines:

- Allow adequate time for negotiating homework.
- Introduce the idea that practising between sessions is important.
- Negotiate rather than impose activities.
- Ensure that the activities are realistic.
- Ensure that your helpee knows precisely what to do.
- Get the instructions written down accurately.
- Discuss potential difficulties in completing agreed-upon activities.
- Signal a joint progress review.

Afterwards hold a sharing and discussion session focusing on your use of negotiating homework skills. If necessary, practise some more until you consider that you have obtained some degree of competence in negotiating homework. Then, if feasible, reverse roles.

Activity 21.2   Identifying supports and resources

For the helpee population(s) with whom you either work or might work in future, identify:

1 What kinds of people might support their attempts to change?
2 What kinds of non-human resources (for instance, audio or video recordings or self-help books) might support their attempts to change?

CONDUCTING MIDDLE SESSIONS

22

CHAPTER GOALS

By studying and doing the activity in this chapter you should:

* Know about the four stages of middle sessions.
* Be able to start conducting middle sessions.

This chapter is relevant to those helpers who either use or are likely to use counselling skills in settings where it is possible to conduct a series of formal helping sessions. Nevertheless, I hope that those of you who use counselling skills in either informal helping contacts or as part of other primary roles can also find something of value in it. The focus here is on middle sessions, those that take place after the initial session and before the last session. If anything, the following review focuses more on conducting sessions in the improving communications/actions and thoughts approach than the facilitating problem-solving approach to the changing stage of the Relating–Understanding–Changing (RUC) helping model. However, many points are relevant to both approaches.

Helping sessions have four phases: preparing, starting, middle and ending. In Box 22.1, based on the assumption that helping will continue for at least one more session, some relevant skills are listed for each phase.

BOX 22.1   THE FOUR PHASES OF HELPING SESSIONS AND THEIR ILLUSTRATIVE SKILLS

1 THE PREPARING PHASE

Reflecting on previous and next session(s)

Consulting with trainers, supervisors and peers

Understanding how to improve the targeted communications/actions and thoughts

(Continued)

(Continued)

Arriving on time

Setting up the room

Relaxing yourself

2 THE STARTING PHASE

Meeting, greeting and seating

Re-establishing the collaborative relationship

Reviewing homework

Establishing session agendas

3 THE MIDDLE PHASE

Actively involving helpees in the change process

Coaching, demonstrating and rehearsing

Checking helpees' understanding

Refining session agendas

Keeping sessions moving

4 THE ENDING PHASE

Structuring to allow time for ending

Reviewing sessions

Negotiating homework

Arranging subsequent contact

THE PREPARING PHASE

Adequate preparation of helping sessions is very important. Arrive either early or, at least, on time for sessions, make sure the room is in order, check any recording equipment they might use and, if necessary, relax yourself. In most instances do not allow helpees into the interview room before you are ready to devote your full attention to them.

Where appropriate, supervisors, trainers and colleagues can assist you to review the previous session to gain insights into how you might approach the next one. In addition, you can revise any strategies you intend using in order to understand their content thoroughly. If necessary, also practise delivering the strategies. Furthermore, you can use between-session time to ensure that you have any written material, such as handouts and home-work forms, readily available. However, avoid being too rigid in approaching sessions, since consulting with helpees is part of establishing a good col-laborative relationship.

THE STARTING PHASE

The starting phase has three main tasks: re-establishing a collaborative rela-tionship, reviewing homework, and establishing a session agenda. Once helpees are comfortably seated, sometimes they will start talking of their own accord. However, on most occasions, you need to make an opening statement. Sample opening statements are provided in Box 22.2. I advocate a 'softly, softly' approach that starts by checking 'where they're at' rather than by moving directly into improving behaviour. Allow helpees the psy-chological safety and space to bring you up to date with information that they select as important from their internal frames of reference.

Once you have allowed helpees air time, you may still require further information to help you to assess how they have progressed in any home-work negotiated in the previous session. Box 22.2 provides some statements that you might make, if you have not already reviewed progress in doing the homework. As appropriate, ask additional questions that clarify and expand your own and their understanding of how they are progressing. Furthermore, encourage them to acknowledge their conscious involvement, or personal agency, in bringing about positive changes during homework. For example, Mustafa, 32, is working with his helper to improve his skills of expressing affection to his partner Yasmin, 31, more openly. Yasmin recently told Mustafa that she thinks they are getting on better. Mustafa's helper encour-ages him to acknowledge that by changing his behaviour, for instance not holding back in telling Yasmin that he loves her and kissing her warmly, he has helped to bring about the improvement. Mustafa might now say to himself 'When I use my self-disclosure skills and am more open in stating and showing my love for Yasmin, I can improve my relationship with her.'

Near the start of each session in the changing stage, consult with the helpee to establish a session agenda. Such agendas may be for all or part of sessions. For example, together you may decide what you will work on first and then, later, make another decision regarding what to work on next. Alternatively, as part of the initial agenda-setting discussion, you may tar-get one area to start and then agree to move on to another area. However, be flexible once you establish session agendas, so that you can respond to emerging developments during sessions.

When establishing session agendas, I favour paying considerable attention to helpees' wishes, since I want to encourage their motivation and involvement. If I thought there was some important reason for starting with a particular improving communication or thoughts goal, I would share this observation. However, I would still be inclined to allow helpees the final say in determining the agenda. Box 22.2 illustrates the kind of agenda-setting statement that you might make near the start of second sessions. Session agendas for later sessions tend to be heavily influenced by the work done and homework negotiated in the previous session.

BOX 22.2   SOME EXAMPLES OF STARTING PHASE STATEMENTS

OPENING STATEMENTS

'How's your week been?'

'How have you been getting on?'

'Where would you like to start today?'

REVIEWING HOMEWORK

'What progress did you make with your homework?'

'What happened when you tried out your changed thoughts/communications?'

'Things didn't just happen: you made them happen by changing (specify what).'

ESTABLISHING A SESSION AGENDA – HELPER TO FATHER

In our first session we stated two mind skills goals for getting on better with Nick (12-year-old son): namely, challenging and then changing your demanding rule that 'Nick never be rude to his mother', and assessing and, if possible, changing your perception that 'Nick never does anything around the house'. We also stated some goals for improving the verbal, vocal and body message components for how you might communicate better with Nick at mealtimes. Which would you like to work on first?

THE MIDDLE PHASE

Once session agendas are established, however informally, helpers can use strategies to assist helpees to attain one or more goals. One way of viewing this middle phase is that it is the working phase of the session.

However, I have not used the term working phase because it may detract from valuable work performed in the preparing, starting and ending phases.

Already, I have emphasized the importance of helpee-centred coaching when assisting helpees to improve their skills. In the middle phase, involve helpees in choices that take place when working on specific skills; for instance how many rehearsals they require to develop targeted verbal, vocal and body messages. Furthermore, involve them in choices about moving on to different items in their session agendas and refining agendas as appropriate. Together, you may make trade-offs and compromises regarding spending session time, for instance, curtailing time spent in one mind skill's or communication skill's area so that you have time available for another.

Keep helping sessions moving at an appropriate pace, neither too fast nor too slow. There are risks in both directions. On the one hand, you may rush through delivering helping strategies in ways that confuse helpees and leave them little to take away after a session's end. Furthermore, you may put too much pressure on them to reveal themselves and to work at an uncongenial pace.

On the other hand, you may allow 'session drift' – sessions that drift along rather aimlessly with little tangible outcome being achieved. Sometimes session drift occurs because helpers are poor at balancing relationship and task considerations, at the expense of the latter. You may need to develop assertiveness skills to curtail long and unproductive conversations. Furthermore, you require a repertoire of checking-out and moving-on statements. Box 22.3 provides examples of such statements.

Though the responsibility should be shared, ultimately it is your responsibility to see that session time is allocated productively. Be careful not to make moving-on statements that allow insufficient time to deal with the next agenda items properly. Generally, it is best to avoid getting into new areas towards the end of sessions rather than to start working on them in rushed and hurried ways.

BOX 22.3   EXAMPLES OF STATEMENTS FOR THE MIDDLE AND ENDING PHASES

MIDDLE PHASE STATEMENTS

Do you want to spend more time now working in this area or are you ready to move on?

I sense that we've taken working on changing your _____ [specify] as far as we can for now. What do you think?

(Continued)

(Continued)

Do you want another rehearsal for communicating better in that situation or do you think you can manage all right?

ENDING PHASE STATEMENTS

I notice that we have to end in about 10 minutes ... and, assuming you want to come here again, perhaps we should spend some of this time looking at what you might do before our next meeting.

Before we end, it might be a good idea to review what we've done today and see how you can build upon it before we next meet.

Is there anything you would like to bring up before we end?

THE ENDING PHASE

There are various tasks involved in ending sessions skilfully in the changing stage of the RUC helping model. Helpers need to bring closure to any work on a targeted skill in process during the middle phase. You may want either yourself or your helpee to review the session. If helpees have not done so already, this may be an opportunity for them to write down their main learnings. In addition, leave sufficient time to negotiate and clarify any homework that they will undertake. Furthermore, discuss and be clear about arrangements for the next session.

To allow time to perform the tasks of the ending phase properly, often it is a good idea to make an early structuring statement that allows for a smooth transition from the middle to the ending phase of the session. You might make such a statement about 5 to 10 minutes before the end of a 45-minute session. The first two ending phase statements in Box 22.3 are examples of statements that helpers might make in this regard.

Sometimes, reviewing sessions assists helpees to clarify and consolidate what they have learned in them. However, session reviews are not always necessary, especially if together you have worked thoroughly during the session. Furthermore, when you negotiate homework you may cover some of the same ground anyway.

In the previous chapter, I mentioned some ways of increasing compliance in performing homework activities. At risk of repetition, these ways include negotiating them rather than imposing them, checking that helpees clearly know how to enact the changed thoughts and communications, writing activities instructions and key points down, and discussing any difficulties that helpees anticipate in carrying out the activities.

When ending sessions, you may also check whether helpees have any unfinished business, queries or outstanding items that they would like to mention. Some helpers like to check how helpees have experienced the session and whether they have any feedback they would like to share. Last, make clear agreements about whether and when you are next going to meet. You may also wish to tell vulnerable 'at risk' helpees under what circumstances and how they can contact you between sessions.

Activity 22.1 Practising conducting second sessions

Work with a partner. Partner A acts as a helper and partner B as the helpee. The helpee chooses a problem situation of relevance to her/him. Assume that you have conducted an initial session and have completed the first two stages of the Relating–Understanding–Changing helping model. Furthermore, assume that together you have identified at least one communication/action and at least one thought to be improved during the changing stage, which may last for at least one more session after this one. Since this is not a real second session, you will need to discuss how each of you can best get into your roles.

Then conduct a second helping session consisting of the following four phases:

- a preparing phase (this may include addressing issues connected with your respective roles)
- a starting phase
- a middle phase
- an ending phase.

Afterwards hold a sharing and feedback discussion. Then, if appropriate, change roles and repeat this activity.

Using audio or video recording and playback may add value to the activity.

ENDING HELPING 23

CHAPTER GOALS

By studying and doing the activities in this chapter you should:

* Know about considerations for when to end helping.
* Have some different formats for ending helping.
* Learn some ways of assisting helpees to maintain changes.

This chapter deals with issues connected with ending helping and conducting final sessions. As with the previous chapter it is mainly based on the assumption that helpers have the opportunity to work with helpees over a series of sessions – say three or more. Again, I hope those of you for whom this assumption does not hold, because of the different nature of your contacts, are able to gain something of value from the discussion.

WHEN TO END

Within the Relating–Understanding–Changing model, when do helpers end the helping process? Sometimes helpees may end of their own accord before helpers think they are ready. Though this may be either because of a helper–helpee mismatch or because helpers demonstrated insufficient skill to have them return, this is not necessarily the case. Helpees may have found their session or sessions with you of value, but think they can continue on their own. Sometimes, external circumstances, such as a change of job or illness, may prevent them continuing. In addition, some may just resist the ideas of having to change and of being in helping.

Many problem situations have their own time frames. When assisting helpees handle specific future events, they may only wish to continue up until that event. In informal helping, contact may end when helpees leave settings, such as hospitals and residential units for juvenile delinquents. On other occasions, helping may end when helpees have made sufficient progress in either the facilitating problem-solving or the improving communications/actions and thoughts approaches to the third stage of the Relating–Understanding–Changing (RUC) helping model. In addition, helping may end as stated in a contract that stipulates the number of sessions it will last.

The following are four main sources of information that you and helpees can use in reviewing when to end helping. First, there is information from what helpees report about their feelings and progress. Are they happy with progress and do they feel they can cope better? Second, there are your own observations about helpees' progress. Third, there is feedback from significant others in helpees' lives, for instance spouses, bosses or peers. Sometimes this feedback goes direct to helpees and then gets relayed to you. Last, you and helpees may end helping on the basis of evidence of attaining measurable goals. An example might be that of a single mother and her teenage son, previously in conflict, who report having 10 minutes of 'happy talk' each day for a week, the son mowing the lawn as agreed, and the mother expressing love and appreciation at least once each day.

FORMATS FOR ENDING HELPING

Sometimes helpers and helpees have limited choice over when to end. Such instances include when leaving town, when terms end, and when helping addresses specific forthcoming situations, such as important examinations or a divorce hearing. On other occasions, you and your helpees have more choice about when to end. The following are some possible formats for ending helping.

- *Fixed ending* You and your helpees may have contracts that you work for, say, eight sessions in one or more problem or problematic skills areas. Advantages of fixed ending include lessening the chance of dependency and motivating helpees. Potential disadvantages include restricting coverage of problems and insufficient thoroughness in training to improve specific skills.
- *Open ending when goals are attained* With open ending, helping concludes when together you agree that the helpee has made sufficient progress in attaining their main goals. Such goals include managing specific problems better and developing improved skills to address current and future problems.
- *Faded ending* Here, the withdrawal of helping assistance is gradual. For example, instead of meeting weekly, the final sessions could be at fortnightly or monthly intervals.
- *Ending with booster session(s)* Booster sessions, say after three months, are not to teach new skills, but to check helpees' progress in consolidating skills, motivate them, and help them work through difficulties in taking away and using trained skills in their home environments.
- *Scheduling follow-up contact after ending* You can schedule follow-up phone calls or postal and e-mail correspondence. Such phone calls and correspondence perform some of the same functions as booster sessions.

ASSISTING MAINTAINING CHANGE

Issues surrounding maintaining changes in problem situations should not be left to final sessions. You can assist helpees to maintain changes during helping by: identifying the key mind and communication skills they need to develop; training thoroughly; and negotiating relevant homework that helps them to transfer what they have learned inside helping to problem situations outside.

During helping, you may make statements indicating its finiteness, for instance, comments about the usefulness of homework for developing improved skills for use when helping ends. Such comments may encourage helpees to make the most of their regular sessions and the time between them. You can also introduce the topic of ending with one or more transition statements that clearly signal that helping is coming to an end. Box 23.1 provides examples of such transition statements.

BOX 23.1 EXAMPLES OF TRANSITION STATEMENTS FOR ENDING HELPING

We only have a few more sessions left. Perhaps we should not only discuss an agenda for this session, but also think about how best we can spend our remaining time together.

Our next session is the final session. Would it be all right with you if we spent some time discussing how to help you retain and build on your improved skills for managing your problem?

Perhaps the agenda for this final session should mainly be how to help you use the skills you've learned here for afterwards. For instance, we can review how much you've changed, where there is still room for improvement, how you might go about it, and plan how to deal with any difficult situations you anticipate.

The main task in ending helping is to assist clients to consolidate what they have learned so that they may continue to help themselves afterwards. One method of enhancing consolidation is for either you or the helpee to summarize the main points learned for dealing with problem situations in future. In addition, you and helpees can spend time anticipating difficulties and setbacks and develop strategies for dealing with them. Some of these strategies may be focused on communication, for instance, how to seek support during attempts to handle a difficult problem situation better.

You can stress the importance of helpees understanding that often they can retrieve mistakes and always they can learn from them. Together, you can develop appropriate self-talk statements for retrieving lapses and get them written down on reminder cards. Furthermore, you can prevent discouragement by distinguishing between a process success and an outcome success: even though they have used good skills in a problem situation (a process success) they may not get what they want (an outcome success). Not getting what they want does not negate the fact that they still performed competently and can do so again in future.

In addition, where appropriate, you can challenge helpees' demanding rules that 'change must be easy' and 'maintaining change must be effortless'. Encourage them to replace such rules with more preferential rules stressing that changing and maintaining change can involve effort, practice and overcoming obstacles. You can also emphasize their assuming personal responsibility for continuing to cope with their problem situations to the best of their ability.

Sometimes it is appropriate to explore, with helpees, arrangements for continuing support. Such support may take the form of identifying and using supportive people, referral to another helper, attending a helping group or training course, self-help reading, and self-help audio or video recordings. In addition, as mentioned previously, you can offer review and booster sessions.

FURTHER ENDING HELPING TASKS AND SKILLS

In addition to the major task of consolidating improved behaviours, there are other tasks when ending helping. How helpers handle them varies with length of helping, the nature of the problem(s) and problematic skills, and the helper–helpee relationship.

DEALING WITH FEELINGS

Helpees' feelings about ending helping fall into two main categories: feelings about how they are going to fare without helpers and feelings towards helpers and the helping process. Often they have feelings of ambivalence about how they will cope after helping. On the one hand, they feel more competent, yet on the other hand they still have doubts about their abilities to implement skills. You can facilitate open discussion of their feelings about the future. Looking at how best to maintain skills also addresses the issue of their lingering doubts. Other helpees will feel confident that they can cope now on their own, which is hopefully a sign of work well done.

Allow helpees the opportunity to share feelings about their contact with you. You may obtain valuable feedback about how you come across and also their reactions to different aspects of the helping process. You may humanize ending by sharing some of your feelings: for instance, 'I enjoyed working with you', or 'I admire the courage with which you face your situation', or 'I'm delighted with your progress.'

ENDING HELPING ETHICALLY

Aim to say goodbye in a business-like, yet friendly way, appropriate to professional rather than personal relationships. By ending helping sloppily, you may undo some of your influence in assisting helpees to maintain their skills.

There are a number of important ethical issues surrounding ending helping. For example, you need to think through your responsibility to helpees after helping. Too much support may engender dependency, too little may fail to carry out 'professional' obligations. Each case must be judged on its merits. Another ethical issue is what you should do when you think helpees have other problems on which they need to work. I suggest the possibility of tactfully bringing such views to their attention.

A further set of ethical issues surrounds the boundaries between personal and professional relationships. Most professional associations have ethical codes about providing counselling and helping services. Helpers who allow their personal and professional wires to get crossed when ending are not only acting unethically, but can make it more difficult for helpees to be assisted by them if future need arises.

EVALUATING COUNSELLING SKILLS

When helping ends, you have many sources of information for evaluating your counselling skills. These sources of information include attendance, intentional and unintentional feedback from helpees, perceptions of helpee progress, session notes, possibly video or audio recordings of helping sessions, helpees' compliance and success in carrying out homework, and feedback from third parties such as supervisors.

You can make a final evaluation of your work with each helpee soon after ending regular contact. Questions to ask include: 'To what extent did the helpee manage her/his problem(s) better and improve their skills?' and 'How well did I use the skills for each stage of the Relating–Understanding–Changing model?' If you defer performing such an evaluation for too long, you risk forgetting valuable information. When evaluating your counselling skills, be aware of any of your characteristic perceiving errors, for example, you may be too hard or too easy on yourself. What you seek is a balanced appraisal of your good and poor skills to guide your future work.

Activity 23.1   Considerations in ending helping

1 Critically discuss the importance and validity of each of the following considerations for when helping should end:

- helpee self-report
- helper observations
- third-party feedback
- attainment of measurable goals
- other factors not mentioned above.

2 Critically discuss the merits of each of the following formats for ending helping:

- fixed ending decided in the initial session
- open ending negotiated between helpee and helper.

3 Critically discuss the value of each of the following ways of assisting helpees to maintain their improved behaviours:

- summarizing the main learnings
- anticipating difficulties and setbacks and developing strategies for dealing with them
- focusing on how helpees can think effectively after helping
- exploring arrangements for continuing support
- other ways not mentioned above.

Activity 23.2   Ending a series of helping sessions

Work with the same partner with whom you performed Activity 22.1. Again, partner A acts as a helper and partner B acts as the helpee. For the problem situation worked on in Activity 22.1, assume that you are now in your third and final helping session. Conduct all or part of this final helping session in which you focus on:

- assisting your helpee to maintain changes
- ending helping smoothly
- saying goodbye.

Afterwards hold a sharing and feedback discussion. Then, if appropriate, change roles and repeat this activity.

Using audio or video recording and playback may add value to the activity.

III

FURTHER CONSIDERATIONS

INTRODUCTION TO RELAXATION

CHAPTER GOALS

By studying and doing the activity in this chapter you should:

- Be introduced to progressive and brief muscular relaxation.
- Know about mental relaxation and mindfulness of breathing.

This chapter introduces training helpees in muscular and mental relaxation skills. I acknowledge that some of you will not use these skills with helpees and, if so, can decide now whether or not to move on to the next chapter. Helpees may use relaxation skills both for managing feelings like anger and anxiety and for dealing with problems such as tension headaches, hypertension and insomnia. Relaxation skills may be used alone or as part of more complex procedures.

PROGRESSIVE MUSCULAR RELAXATION

The physical setting where you train helpees should be conducive to relaxation. This involves an absence of disruptive noise, interior decoration that is restful, and lighting which may be dimmed. Helpees can relax in recliner chairs, or on mattresses or, at the very least, in comfortable upright chairs with headrests.

From the start you can teach relaxation as a useful skill for daily life. Furthermore, helpees should understand that success at learning relaxation, just like success at learning any other skill, requires practice and that relaxation homework is necessary. Before starting relaxation, you can suggest that they wear loose-fitting, comfortable clothing both during interviews and when doing relaxation homework, and that it is helpful to remove items such as glasses and shoes.

In training muscular relaxation there is a succession of instructions for each muscle group. You go through a five-step tension–relax cycle for each muscle group. These steps are:

1 *Focus* attention on a particular muscle group
2 *Tense* the muscle group
3 *Hold* – Maintain the tension for five to seven seconds
4 *Release* the tension in the muscle group
5 *Relax* – Spend 20 to 30 seconds focusing on letting go of tension and further relaxing the muscle groups.

Helpees need to learn this *focus–tense–hold–release–relax* cycle so that they may apply it in their homework.

Having explained the basic tension–relax cycle, you may then demonstrate it by going through the cycle in relation to your own right hand and forearm, and at each stage asking the helpee to do the same. Thus, 'I'm focusing all my attention on my right hand and forearm and I'd like you to do the same', progresses to 'I'm clenching my right fist and tensing the muscles in my lower arm …', then on to 'I'm holding my right fist clenched and keeping the muscles in my lower arm tensed …', followed by 'I'm now releasing as quickly as I can the tension from my right fist and lower arm …', ending with 'I'm relaxing my right hand and forearm, letting the tension go further and further and letting these muscles become more and more relaxed …'. The final relaxation phase tends to last from 30 to 60 seconds, frequently accompanied by relaxation 'patter' about letting the tension go and acknowledging and experiencing feelings of deeper and deeper relaxation as this occurs. Especially the first time, having been through the tension–relax cycle once in relation to the right hand and forearm, you may instruct the helpee through it again.

You are then likely to take helpees through various muscle groups, demonstrating them as necessary. Box 24.1 shows 16 muscle groups and suggested tensing instructions. The arms tend to come at the beginning, since they are easy to demonstrate. For most helpees, relaxing parts of the face is particularly important, as the most marked anxiety-inhibiting effects are usually obtained there.

BOX 24.1   RELAXATION TRAINING MUSCLE GROUPS AND TENSING INSTRUCTIONS

Muscle group	Tensing instructions*
Right hand and forearm	Clench your right fist and tense the muscles in your lower arm.
Right biceps	Bend your right arm at the elbow and flex your biceps by tensing the muscles of your upper right arm.

Muscle group	Tensing instructions*
Left hand and forearm	Clench your left fist and tense the muscles in your lower arm.
Left biceps	Bend your left arm at the elbow and flex your biceps by tensing the muscles of your upper left arm.
Forehead	Lift your eyebrows as high as possible.
Eyes, nose and upper cheeks	Squeeze your eyes tightly shut and wrinkle your nose.
Jaw and lower cheeks	Clench your teeth and pull the corners of your mouth firmly back.
Neck and throat	Pull your chin down hard towards your chest yet resist having it touch your chest.
Chest and shoulders	Pull your shoulder blades together and take a deep breath.
Stomach	Tighten the muscles in your stomach as though someone was about to hit you there.
Right thigh	Tense the muscles of the right upper leg by pressing the upper muscle down and the lower muscles up.
Right calf	Stretch your right leg and pull your toes towards your head.
Right foot	Point and curl the toes of your right foot and turn it inwards.
Left thigh	Tense the muscles of the left upper leg by pressing the upper muscle down and the lower muscles up.
Left calf	Stretch your left leg and pull your toes towards your head.
Left foot	Point and curl the toes of your left foot and turn it inwards.

* With left-handed people, tensing instructions for the left side of the body should come before those for the right.

Once helpees have learned how to tense the various muscle groups, instruct them to keep their eyes closed during relaxation training and practice. Towards the end of relaxation sessions, you may ask them for a summary of their relaxation, along the lines of 'Well, how was your relaxation today?', and discuss any issues that arise. Ending relaxation sessions may be achieved by counting from five to one and, when you get to one, asking them to wake up pleasantly relaxed as though from a peaceful sleep.

You can further stress the importance of practising muscular relaxation at the end of the initial relaxation session. Helpees are likely to be given the homework assignment of practising muscular relaxation for one or two 15-minute periods per day. You should ask them whether they anticipate any obstacles to practising, such as finding a quiet place, and help them to devise strategies for ensuring good homework. You can also either make up recordings of relaxation instructions that they can take away for homework purposes or recommend existing relaxation training recordings. There is some evidence that those who record details of their relaxation practice are much more likely to continue doing it. Consequently, it may be helpful to give helpees logs for monitoring their relaxation homework.

BRIEF MUSCULAR RELAXATION

Brief muscular relaxation skills aim to induce deep relaxation with less time and effort than the 16-muscle-group relaxation procedure. When helpees are proficient in full progressive muscular relaxation, you can introduce such skills. Brief relaxation skills are useful both in helping sessions and in daily life. The following are two examples.

SEQUENTIAL BRIEF RELAXATION

Here, you can first instruct helpees and then get them to give themselves the following instructions, focused on tensing and relaxing four composite muscle groupings in turn.

> I'm going to count to ten in units of two. After each unit of two I will instruct you to tense and relax a muscle grouping. One, two … focus on your leg and feet muscles … tense and hold the tension in these muscles for five seconds … release … relax and enjoy the sensations of the tension flowing from your legs and feet. Three, four … take a deep breath and focus on your chest, shoulder and stomach muscles … tense and hold the tension in these muscles for five seconds … release … relax and enjoy the sensations of the tension flowing from your chest, shoulders and stomach. Five, six … focus on your face, neck and head muscles … tense and hold the tension in these muscles for five seconds … release … relax and enjoy the sensations of the tension flowing from your face, neck and head. Seven, eight … focus on your arm and hand muscles … tense and hold the tension in these muscles for five seconds … release … relax and enjoy the sensations of the tension flowing from your arms and hands. Nine, ten … focus on all the muscles in your body … tense all the muscles in your body together and hold for five seconds … release … relax and enjoy the sensations of the tension leaving your whole body as your relaxation gets deeper and deeper … deeper and deeper … deeper and deeper.

SIMULTANEOUS BRIEF RELAXATION

As at the end of the previous example, you can instruct helpees to tense all muscle groupings simultaneously. You can say:

When I give the signal, I would like you to close your eyes very tightly, take a deep breath, and simultaneously tense your arm muscles, your face, neck and throat muscles, your chest, shoulder and stomach muscles, and your leg and foot muscles. Now take a deep breath and tense all your muscles … hold for five seconds … now release and relax as deeply as you can.

MENTAL RELAXATION

You can assist helpees to identify one or more favourite scenes conducive to feeling relaxed. Often they visualize such restful scenes at the end of progressive muscular relaxation. The following is an example of a helper instructing a helpee to mentally relax.

You're lying on an empty beach on a pleasant, sunny day, enjoying the sensations of warmth on your body. There is a gentle breeze. You can hear the peaceful noise of the sea steadily lapping against the shore. You haven't a care in the world, and you enjoy your feelings of peace and calm, peace and calm, peace and calm, and your feelings of relaxation and wellbeing.

Helpees can visualize mental relaxation scenes independent of muscular relaxation. In addition, they can use the 'counting to ten in groups of two' as a mental relaxation rather than as a muscular relaxation procedure. For example: 'One, two … focus on your leg and feet muscles … relax and enjoy the sensations of the tension flowing from your legs and feet.' As a mental relaxation procedure, helpees edit out the 'tense, hold and release' instructions.

Using coaching, demonstrating and rehearsing, you can train helpees to develop mental relaxation procedures as self-help skills. They may wish to record their self-instructions for playback outside of helping sessions.

MINDFULNESS OF BREATHING

Some helpers may wish to train helpees in mindfulness of breathing. Focusing attention on breathing is possibly the most universal of meditative practices in the world and is also the starting point of Buddhist mind training. In Eastern countries, the lotus posture with fully crossed legs is most commonly adopted for breathing meditation. Westerners not wanting to use this position can sit upright in a relatively comfortable chair with their legs slightly apart and feet firmly placed on the floor. The hands of those meditating are generally cupped on their laps, most usually with the left hand being placed palm up below the right, which is also palm up. Alternatively, the hands may be placed face down on the knees. When attending to their breathing, helpees may close their eyes to prevent the mind being distracted by what is seen. Some people, however, when focusing on breathing for extended periods of time prefer to keep their eyes slightly open to avoid drowsiness. One option here is to then focus on the tip of your nose and attempt to be oblivious to all other things.

Teach helpees that the main task in mindfulness of breathing is to concentrate on the natural flow of the breath – breathing in, breathing out, breathing in, breathing out and so on – to establish concentrated awareness. The nose is the starting point of the in-breath, the chest the middle, and the abdomen the end. While breathing out, the reverse is the case. Those engaging in mindfulness of breathing can follow the process of their breaths through these stages of breathing in and breathing out. Either after or instead of doing this, helpees can establish a check point, with the nose-tip being most recommended, and fix their attention there where the breaths are sure to pass in and out. One variation on mindfulness of breathing is to accompany each out-breath by gently and sub-vocally saying 'calm' to yourself. Another variation is to accompany successive in-breaths by quietly and sub-vocally counting from one to nine, then down to one, then up again to nine, and so on.

When starting to learn mindfulness of breathing and even when more experienced in it, people's minds meander into extraneous thoughts or fantasies, be they past, present or future. On such occasions, helpees can be taught gently to bring their minds back to focusing on their next breath. They should not worry if they repeatedly have to bring themselves back to being aware of their breathing. Analogies that are sometimes used for training in mindfulness of breathing are those of training a puppy or a calf. At the end of a mindfulness-of-breathing session, helpees who have closed their eyes should gently reopen them.

RELAXATION TRAINING CONSIDERATIONS

Helpers differ in the number of sessions they use for relaxation training. Furthermore, helpees differ in the speed with which they attain a capacity to relax. The late Dr Joseph Wolpe, a noted pioneer of behaviour therapy, taught progressive muscular relaxation in about six lessons and asked his patients to practise at home for two 15-minute sessions per day. He considered that it was crucial for clients to realize that the aim of relaxation training was not muscle control per se, but emotional calmness. You may vary your relaxation training timetable according to helpees' needs and your own workload. Nevertheless, it is important that they have sufficient sessions to learn relaxation adequately. Furthermore, they need to practise their relaxation skills diligently and review progress with you. In addition, it benefits many to integrate relaxation skills into their daily lives.

Activity 24.1 Training a helpee in relaxation

Conduct a helping session in which partner A's task is to train partner B, who acts as helpee in progressive muscular relaxation skills. During the session, partner A:

- offers reasons for using progressive muscular relaxation;
- provides a live demonstration of tensing and relaxing the first muscle grouping in Box 24.1;
- makes up a progressive muscular relaxation recording as s/he relaxes partner B using the five-step tension–relax cycle;
- presents a mental relaxation scene at the end of the muscular relaxation;
- checks how relaxed the helpee becomes and provides further relaxation instructions for any muscle group where s/he still feels tense; and
- negotiates with the helpee a progressive muscular relaxation homework practice assignment.

Afterwards both partners hold a sharing and discussion session and, if feasible, reverse roles.

MANAGING CRISES

CHAPTER GOALS

By studying and doing the activity in this chapter you should:

- Know when helpees are in crisis.
- Possess some skills for managing helpees in crisis.

Though helping trainees should not at first be faced with helpees in crisis, this cannot be guaranteed. Sometimes the fact that helpees are in crisis becomes apparent at the start of initial sessions, but this is not always the case. Otherwise you may have to deal with helpees in crisis outside of formal settings. In crisis helping, you are faced with making immediate choices to assist helpees to get through their sense of being overwhelmed. Some of these choices may also help them to manage better any underlying problems contributing to the crisis.

DEFINING CRISES

Crises may be defined as situations of excessive stress. Stress tends to have a negative connotation in our culture. This is unjustified if you think of stress in terms of challenges in life. Each person has an optimum stress level or a particular level of stimulation at which they feel comfortable. At this level they may experience what might be termed 'stress without distress'. Beneath this level they may feel insufficiently stimulated and bored. Above this level they are likely to experience physiological and psychological distress. If the heightened stress is prolonged or perceived as extremely severe, helpees may feel that their coping resources are inadequate to meet the demands being made upon them. In such circumstances they are in situations of excessive stress or are in states of crisis.

This chapter, on handling crises, relates mainly to helpees who are in fairly acute states of distress. At this juncture they may be experiencing heightened or maladaptive reactions in a number of different, though inter-related, areas.

PHYSICAL REACTIONS

Physical reactions may include hypertension and proneness to such things as heart attacks and gastric ulcers. The weakest parts of different helpees' bodies tend to be most adversely affected by stress.

FEELINGS

Feelings associated with excessive stress include shock, depression, frustration, anger, anxiety, disorientation and fears of nervous breakdown or insanity.

THOUGHTS

Some of the main thoughts associated with excessive stress are that helpees are powerless to make a positive impact on their situations, that things are getting out of control, and thoughts associated with despair and lack of hope for the future. The notion of excessive stress can imply that their thought processes have become somewhat irrational. They think ineffectively – for example, with tunnel vision involving focusing on only a few factors in a situation.

COMMUNICATION/ACTIONS

Avoidance and overactivity are two of the main ways in which helpees handle excessive stress. Their behaviour may range from giving up and not making an effort, to rigid, repetitive and frenetic attempts to deal with their problems. Violence, either self-inflicted or turned outwards, is more likely at times of excessive stress than when stress levels are lower.

It is very important that you realize that crises, however large or small they may appear from outsiders' frames of reference, tend to seem overwhelming from insiders' frames of reference. Some crises simmer in the background for a long time and suddenly erupt, whereas others are more clearly a reaction to an immediate precipitating event, for instance a bereavement or loss of a job. Perhaps many stressful situations only really turn into psychological crises at the point where helpees feel that their efforts to adapt and cope are totally insufficient. There are numerous situations which may cause helpees to feel that they are at the limit of their coping resources, though there are wide differences in people's abilities to tolerate these various stressors. Resilience in the face of stress depends partly on personal resources and skills. However, it may also be heavily influenced by the amount of family, social and community support available.

GUIDELINES FOR CRISIS COUNSELLING AND HELPING

Crises for helpees can be crises for helpers too. You may feel under great pressure to relieve helpees' distress at the same time as being threatened by the strength of their emotions. Below are suggested some guidelines for crisis helping.

BE PREPARED

Those responsible for helpees can relieve much stress if it is realized that, since these events are likely to be part of any helper's life, it is best to be prepared. One way of preparing is to ensure that you can quickly mobilize a good support system, for example, a competent physician or a bed in a psychiatric hospital. You can also prepare for crises by being clear about the limit of your responsibility for clients.

ACT CALMLY

Even though it may seem a limitation on being genuine, it is important that you act calmly. You should not add your anxieties to clients' agitation and distress. Responding in warm yet firm and measured ways may both give helpees the security of feeling assisted by a strong person and also calm their heightened emotions.

LISTEN AND OBSERVE

A major reason that stressful situations become crises for many helpees is that they feel that they have no one to whom they can turn who will listen to and understand their difficulties. They may become calmer and feel less isolated and despairing simply by being able to share their problems and air the related emotions with you. Catharsis is another word for this process of letting out pent-up feelings. Listening, observing and empathic respond-ing can help you to understand their worlds as well as contributing to their feelings of being heard and accepted.

ASSESS SEVERITY AND RISK OF DAMAGE TO SELF AND TO OTHERS

One area of assessing severity concerns the degree to which helpees are in contact with reality. Assessing risk may also mean assessing the damage they may do to other people. However, it is more likely to involve assessing the damage that they may do to themselves, including committing suicide.

A high proportion of suicidal people talk about the possibility before making any attempt. Be sensitive about picking up cries for help and not allowing anxiety to interfere with your listening skills. Suicidal people are often ambivalent about doing it. A caring question about whether or not they are considering suicide may be very appropriate. Avoidance or dealing with the topic indirectly may sometimes increase rather than diminish risk.

ASSESS HELPEES' STRENGTHS AND COPING SKILLS

You can both assess and assist helpees to explore and assess their strengths and coping skills. Often in crises they are so overwhelmed by negative thinking that they allow themselves to forget their strengths. While not advocating superficial reassurance, the following remarks may be helpful to certain helpees in some situations: 'Well, we've explored your problems in some detail. I'm now wondering whether you feel that you have any strengths or resources for dealing with them?', 'You've been telling me a lot about negative aspects of your life. Can you tell me if there are any positive aspects as well?' and 'As you talk you seem to be facing your problems very much on your own. I'm wondering whether there are any friends, relatives or other people who might be available to offer you some support.'

ASSIST EXPLORATION AND CLARIFICATION OF PROBLEM(S)

Helpees in crises have often lost perspective on themselves and their problems. One reason for this is that crises involve very intense feelings. Until some progress is made in dealing with relieving the intensity of feelings, they may have insufficient ability to be rational about the factors generating their strong emotions. Skills that you can use during the work of exploring and clarifying problems are likely to include empathic responding, use of questions, summarizing, and challenging any distortions in thinking that make their lives seem hopeless.

ASSIST PROBLEM-MANAGEMENT AND PLANNING

A primary emphasis in crisis helping is to assist helpees to regain some sense of control over their lives. For some the opportunity to talk with an understanding person may give them enough confidence in their ability to cope with life to move out of the danger zone. With others, your role will include helping them to develop strategies for coping with their immediate distress and, where appropriate, initiating ways and skills for dealing with their longer-term problems. If they are at any risk, plans for coping with immediate situations should be formulated as specifically as possible. For example:

'We have agreed that you will stay at your sister's tonight and that we will meet at 11 am tomorrow. Do you think there is any reason why you can't do this?'

Assisting problem-management and planning may involve mobilizing additional resources, who may be either professional helpers, such as doctors and priests, or friends and relatives. In some instances it is best for helpees to take responsibility for making contact, but not invariably. You always need to assess what is in their best interests and, at highly vulnerable times in their lives, act accordingly.

BE SPECIFIC ABOUT AVAILABILITY

Part of a crisis management plan with certain helpees may be to give them the security of another appointment or meeting with you in the near future. In addition, where relevant, attention needs to be paid to the matter of between-session contact. If such contact seems appropriate, you can say something along the lines of 'If you feel you need me in an emergency, please don't hesitate to get in touch with me either here or on my mobile phone. The numbers are _____.' In most instances they will not get in touch. However, your willingness to be contacted can reassure distressed helpees.

Apparently the Chinese use two symbols for the concept of crisis: one for danger and another for opportunity. Crises can be the impetus for certain helpees to work hard on problems that have been simmering in the past, yet which have to date not been properly confronted. At best, crises can give both of you the opportunity to form an effective relationship. Such relationships can provide the basis for helpees to develop confidence and skills either to prevent or to cope better with future crises.

Activity 25.1   Crisis counselling and helping skills

1   Identify, with regard to your present or future counselling and helping work, the kinds of stressors that bring or may in future bring helpees in crisis to see you.
2   Counsel or help a partner, who role-plays a helpee in crisis. As far as possible, keep in mind the following guidelines:

- act calmly
- listen and observe
- assess severity and risk of damage to self and others
- assess helpee strengths and coping skills
- assist exploring and clarifying problems
- assist problem-management and planning
- be specific about your availability.

Afterwards, discuss and reverse roles.

ETHICAL ISSUES AND DILEMMAS

All helpers develop personal systems of ethics for how they work with helpees. Ethical codes or ethical guidelines for counselling and helping attempt to present acceptable standards for practice. Sometimes it is obvious when there has been an ethical lapse, for instance engaging in sexual relations with clients. However, in the complexities of helping practice, ethical issues often are unclear. Consequently, you are faced with ethical dilemmas involving choices about how best to act.

ETHICAL ISSUES AND DILEMMAS IN HELPING PRACTICE

Ethical issues and dilemmas permeate helping practice. To use legal language, you always have a duty of care to your helpees. Virtually everything you do as a helper can be performed ethically or unethically. Here I group ethical issues and dilemmas connected with enacting this duty of care into four main areas, albeit overlapping:

• helper competence
• helpee autonomy
• confidentiality
• helpee protection.

HELPER COMPETENCE

With so many approaches to helping, the issue arises as to what competence is. A useful distinction exists between relationship competence (offering a good helping relationship) and technical competence (the ability to assess helpees and to deliver interventions). There is far greater agreement between the different helping approaches on the ingredients of relationship competence, such as respect and support for helpees as persons and accurately listening to and understanding their worldviews, than there is for technical competence. Suffice it for now to say that technical competence is what leading practitioners in a given approach would agree to be competent performance of the technical aspects of that approach.

Another helpful distinction is that between readiness to practise and fitness to practise. Readiness to practise means that you require appropriate training and practice before you are ready to see helpees and to use your counselling skills competently. Fitness to practise assumes that you have satisfactory counselling skills in your repertoire and it only becomes an ethical problem when you are precluded in some way from using these skills competently. An example of readiness to practise as an ethical problem is if you take on cases referred to you, for example anorexic helpees, that are beyond your level of training and competence. An example of fitness to practise as an ethical problem is if you were to drink at work and so fail to maintain competence.

You can avoid ethical issues concerning readiness to practise if you are prepared to refer certain helpees on to others more qualified to help them. Furthermore, where you do not possess the requisite competence to help some categories of helpees, discourage colleagues from referring such people to you.

You also have a responsibility to current and future helpees to keep monitoring your performance and developing your counselling skills. Always take care to evaluate and reflect upon what you do. In addition, where possible, it is desirable to receive either supervision or consultative support to gain insight into good skills and pinpoint skills that you can improve.

HELPEE AUTONOMY

Respect for the helpees, right to make the choices that work best for them in their lives is the principle that underlies helpee self-determination. Seek to support helpees' control over and ability to assume personal responsibility for their lives. If you were, for example, to provide inaccurate pre-helping information or make false statements about your professional qualifications and competence, you would stop potential and actual helpees from making informed choices about whether to commence and/or continue in helping with you.

Most often it is unnecessary and unrealistic to provide lengthy explanations about what you do. Nevertheless, before and during helping, make accurate statements concerning the helping process and about your respective roles. Furthermore, answer queries about helping honestly and with respect.

In addition make realistic statements about the outcomes of helping, and avoid making claims that might be disputed both outside and inside of law courts. Throughout helping, treat helpees as intelligent participants who have a right to explanations about why you suggest strategies and what is entailed in implementing them.

An issue in helpee autonomy is where the values and backgrounds of helpees may differ from those of their helpers, for instance as a result of cultural or religious influences. You should not impose your values, and, where appropriate, be prepared to refer helpees on to other helpers who may more readily understand their concerns. It is highly unethical to assess and treat helpees as pathological on the basis of judgments determined by culture, race, sex or sexual orientation, among other characteristics.

CONFIDENTIALITY

Sometimes it is said that all people have three lives: a public life, a private life and a secret life. Since helping frequently deals with material from helpees' secret lives, their trust that their confidences will be kept is absolutely vital. However, there may be reasons connected with matters such as agency policy and, sometimes, the law, why you cannot guarantee confidentiality. For example, when working with minors – be it in private practice, educational or medical settings – there are many ethical and legal issues surrounding the boundaries of confidentiality and obligations to parents, teachers and significant others.

Try to communicate pertinent limitations on confidentiality in advance. Furthermore, other than in exceptional circumstances, seek permission for any communication to third parties. Having said this, the issue of whether or not to disclose to third parties is at the forefront of ethical dilemmas for helpers, especially where risks to children are involved. In a study, published in 1999 by British psychologists Geoff Lindsay and the late Petrūska Clarkson, the answers of a sample of psychotherapists' reporting ethically troubling incidents concerning confidentiality fell into the following four areas:

- risk to third parties – sexual abuse
- risk to the helpee – threatened suicide
- disclosure of information to others – particularly to medical agencies, other colleagues, and the helpee's close friends and relatives; and
- careless/inappropriate disclosure – by the psychotherapist or others.

Confidentiality assumes that helpees have the right to control the disclosure of their personal information. In instances where you require recordings for supervision purposes, refrain from putting pressure on helpees to be recorded. Most will understand a tactful request to record and, provided they are assured of the security of the media, will give their permission. In cases where helpees have reservations, they are often reassured if told that they may stop the recording any time they wish.

Helpees' records, whether they are case notes or audio or video recordings, need to be held securely at all times. A final word about confidentiality is that, when talking socially with colleagues, relatives or friends, keep silent about details of helpees' problems and lives. Unfortunately, a few helpers are tempted to break confidentiality for the sake of a good story.

HELPEE PROTECTION

The category of helpee protection encompasses looking after helpees as persons. You require sufficient detachment to act in their best interests. Dual relationships are those where, in addition to the helping relationship, you may already be in, or consider entering, or enter other kinds of relationships with helpees: for instance, friend, lover, colleague, trainer, supervisor, among others. As mentioned in Chapter 1, dual relationships are often part of the fabric of helping relationships where helpers perform other primary roles, for example nurse–patient. Therefore whether a dual helper–helpee relationship is ethical, unethical or presents an ethical dilemma depends on the circumstances of the relationship.

Sexual contact with helpees is always unethical. Instead of or as well as sexual exploitation, helpees may also be subject to emotional and financial exploitation. Emotional exploitation can take many forms, but has the underlying theme of using helpees in some way for your own personal agenda, for example encouraging dependent and admiring helpees rather than fostering autonomy. Financial exploitation can also take many forms, including charging for services that you are unqualified to provide, overcharging and prolonging helping unnecessarily. You need to ensure too that all reasonable precautions are taken to ensure helpees' physical safety.

You can protect helpees and the public image of your profession if you take steps to address the detrimental behaviour of other helpers. Where you suspect misconduct by other helpers, you can be guided by your professional association's codes of ethics and practice. For instance, if you suspect misconduct by another helper, first you may attempt to resolve or remedy it through discussion with the helper concerned. If still dissatisfied, you can implement any complaints procedures provided by your professional association, doing so without breaches of confidentiality other than those being necessary for investigating the complaint.

MAKING DECISIONS ABOUT ETHICAL ISSUES AND DILEMMAS

Professional ethical codes and guidelines are an important source as you develop a personal system of ethics for your helping practice. Examples of professional codes are the British Association for Counselling and Psychotherapy's *Ethical Framework for Good Practice in Counselling and Psychotherapy*, the Psychotherapy and Counselling Federation of Australia's *Introduction to PACFA, A Definition of Psychotherapy and Counselling, Ethical Guidelines* and *Professional Training Standards*, and the American Counseling Association's *ACA Code of Ethics*. Such codes of conduct can provide a starting point for a process of ethical decision making since they lay out what is generally considered good practice for a particular group.

You require both ethical awareness and the skills of ethical decision making. Possessing a systematic step-by-step way of approaching difficult ethical dilemmas may increase your chances of making sound ethical decisions. Box 26.1 shows the ethical problem-solving model of noted British counselling writer Tim Bond.

BOX 26.1   BOND'S ETHICAL PROBLEM-SOLVING MODEL

- Produce a brief description of the problem or dilemma.
- Decide 'Whose dilemma is it anyway?'
- Consider all available ethical principles and guidelines.
- Identify all possible courses of action.
- Select the best possible course of action.
- Evaluate the outcome.

In light of the emphasis of this book on good and poor mind skills, the Bond model is rather too optimistic in implying that ethical decision making is a rational process. Helpers tend to bring different decision-making styles to ethical decisions: for example, some avoid making them for as long as possible, others rush into making them, still others worry over every detail. In addition, even when helpers make decisions, they differ in their commitment to them and in their abilities to implement them skilfully. Always be alert for how you may be turning what is outwardly a rational decision-making process into one that is less than completely rational because of your own needs and anxieties. Furthermore, the more you can successfully work on your own mental development both as a person and as a helper, the more likely you are to work your way rationally through the ethical dilemmas that inevitably arise in helping.

Activity 26.1   Ethical issues and dilemmas in helping practice

Critically discuss how each of the following areas contains important ethical issues, and possibly dilemmas, for you as a helper.

HELPER COMPETENCE

- relationship competence
- technical competence
- readiness to practise
- fitness to practise
- recognizing limitations and making referrals.

HELPEE AUTONOMY

- respect for helpee self-determination
- accuracy in pre-helping information
- accuracy in statements about professional competence
- honest statements about helping processes and outcomes
- respect for diverse values.

CONFIDENTIALITY

- any limitations communicated in advance
- consent for communication with third parties
- issues of permission and parental involvement with minors
- permission to record sessions
- security of all helpee records.

HELPEE PROTECTION

- maintaining appropriate boundaries to the helping relationship
- avoidance of emotional and sexual exploitation
- protection of helpees' physical safety
- addressing the detrimental behaviour of other helpers.

1 In what areas do you consider yourself most at risk of acting unethically when you help?
2 What can you do to protect your helpees and yourself from your potential to act unethically in the areas you have identified?

Activity 26.2   Making decisions about ethical issues and dilemmas

1 Critically discuss the strengths and weaknesses of Bond's problem-solving model.
2 What can you do to improve your ability to make decisions wisely when faced with ethical issues and dilemmas in future?

MULTICULTURAL AND GENDER AWARE HELPING 27

This chapter provides a brief introduction to diversity-sensitive helping. Addressing the range of differences presented in Chapter 3 is much too vast a topic for a single chapter, especially one in a basic counselling skills book. Consequently, I review selected issues connected with multicultural helping and gender aware helping as being particularly important and relevant for many helpers.

MULTICULTURAL HELPING

MULTICULTURAL HELPING GOALS

In Chapter 3, I provided information on how Britain, Australia and the United States of America are becoming more multicultural. However, Britain already has a large existing population for its relatively small land mass, so it will likely always remain somewhat mono-cultural as well. There are many different groups for whom cultural considerations are important. These include first-generation migrants, descendants of migrants at varying levels of assimilation to the mainstream culture, and members of the mainstream culture, among others. In addition, in Australia, there are the indigenous Aboriginal and Torres Strait Islanders.

Sometimes the goals of multicultural helping are simplified to that of how best to assist minority group members when faced with hostile majority group cultures. In reality, multicultural helping is a much more complex and varied endeavour. Some goals for multicultural helping centre around the period of transition from a previous culture to a new host culture, such as that of Britain and Australia. All migrants require culture-sensitive support to help them adjust and assimilate into their new host cultures. A minority of migrants require specialized help for post-traumatic stress disorders caused by their previous home country and refugee experiences, some of which were horrific.

An issue for migrants and children of migrants is that of handling inter-generational and cross-cultural relationships. For example, value conflicts can exist between migrant parents and their children who adopt more of the values of their new countries. In addition, members of both migrant and mainstream cultures can require help in negotiating cross-cultural inti-mate relationships. You may also need to help some minority group helpees from further marginalizing themselves by unfairly 'demonizing' their host cultures at the same time as doing little positive to change their situations.

Another set of goals for multicultural helping concerns issues of equality, self-respect and coping with discrimination. You can assist helpees to take pride in their culture and race and to liberate themselves from internalized negative stereotypes. Some helpees require support and skills to deal with the inner wounds and outer circumstances of racism. Furthermore, some main-stream culture helpees require assistance in relinquishing negative aspects of their upbringing, such as a false sense of cultural and racial superiority.

MULTICULTURAL COUNSELLING COMPETENCIES

Increasingly, helpers are challenged to develop multicultural counselling competencies. A committee of the American Psychological Association's Division of Counseling Psychology identified multicultural counselling competencies as having three main dimensions: awareness of own assump-tions, values and biases, understanding the worldview of the culturally different client, and developing appropriate strategies and techniques (see Sue et al. (1998) *Multicultural Counseling Competencies,* in the Annotated Bibliography). Each dimension is divided into beliefs and attitudes, knowl-edge and skills. Readers may feel overwhelmed when reading about the proposed multicultural competencies, since it is a counsel of perfection. However, I present a summary of the competencies, with the words helper and helpee substituted for counsellor and client, to indicate some areas that you may need to address when using basic counselling skills with people from different cultures.

AWARENESS OF OWN ASSUMPTIONS, VALUES AND BIASES

The beliefs held by culturally skilled helpers include being sensitive to their own cultural heritage, being comfortable with the differences of helpees from other cultures and races, and recognizing the limitations of their competence and expertise. Helpers should know about their cultural and racial heritage and how this affects the counselling process; understand how oppression, racism and discrimination may affect them personally and in their work; and know about the impact of how they communicate on culturally different helpees. Skills include seeking out relevant educational and training experiences, actively understanding oneself as a cultural and racial being, and seeking an identity that transcends race.

UNDERSTANDING THE WORLDVIEW OF THE CULTURALLY DIFFERENT HELPEE

Beliefs and attitudes for culturally skilled helpers include being aware of their negative emotional reactions and of the stereotypes and preconceived notions that they may hold towards culturally and racially different groups. Helpers should know about the cultural experiences, cultural heritage and historical backgrounds of any particular group with whom they work; acknowledge how culture and race can affect help-seeking behaviour; know how culture and race can influence assessment and the selection and implementation of counselling interventions; and know about the oppressive political and environmental influences impinging on the lives of ethnic and racial minorities. Skills include keeping up-to-date on research findings relevant to the psychological wellbeing of various ethnic and racial groups as well as being actively involved with minorities outside of work settings to gain deeper insight into their perspectives.

DEVELOPING APPROPRIATE INTERVENTION STRATEGIES AND TECHNIQUES

Culturally skilled helpers' attitudes and beliefs include respecting helpees' religious and spiritual beliefs about physical and mental functioning, respecting indigenous helping practices, and valuing bilingualism. Their knowledge base includes understanding how the culture-bound, class-bound and monolingual characteristics of counselling clash with the cultural values of various minority groups; being aware of institutional barriers to minority groups using helping services; knowing about the potential for bias in assessment instruments; and understanding minority group family structures, hierarchies, and community characteristics and resources. Skills include the ability to send and receive verbal and non-verbal communication accurately; interacting in the language requested by helpees or making appropriate referrals; tailoring the counselling relationship and interventions to the helpees' stage of cultural and racial identity development; and engaging in a variety of helping roles beyond those perceived as conventional for counsellors. Such roles include advisor, advocate, change agent and facilitator of indigenous healing and support systems.

As a beginning helper you need to build your skills cumulatively, from the basic to the more advanced. You cannot be expected to have expertise at dealing with a range of culturally different helpees that even many experienced helpers do not possess. Gaining an initial awareness of how cultural considerations can influence basic counselling skills, such as active listening and asking questions, is a good place to start in the process of developing into a genuinely culturally sensitive helper.

GENDER AWARE HELPING

GENDER AWARE HELPING GOALS

Where gender-role issues are involved, it is possible to state helping goals for both sexes and for each sex. Gender aware helping for both sexes involves general goals that include assisting individual helpees to use their strengths and potential, make appropriate choices, remedy poor skills, and develop positive and flexible self-concepts. In addition, helping goals relating to gender roles can often involve both male and female partners: for example, learning to deal with demand/withdraw interaction patterns in marital conflict and handling the numerous issues confronting dual-career couples in a time of rapid technological and economic change.

For a minority, gender aware goals for both sexes can include coming to terms with homosexuality or with varying degrees of bisexuality. This is partly a matter of personal thoughts and feelings, but also a matter of outer behaviour and learning to feel more comfortable with it.

Essential goals for feminist counselling and helping are women valuing themselves on their own terms and women becoming free of sex-role stereotypes. Statements of goals that take women's sex and gender issues into account can focus both on women's life span issues and on problems that are much more commonly faced by women than men. For example, gender aware and feminist helpers can counsel mid-life women to cope with the menopause constructively. In addition, suitably trained and qualified helpers can assist women to address issues such as insufficient assertion, eating disorders, domestic violence and sexual harassment.

Helping goals for men can include addressing excessive need for success, power and competition, restrictive emotionality and restrictive affectionate behaviour between men. Other helping goals include stopping being physically violent both inside and outside of the home, dealing with work-related stress, overcoming tendencies to treat women as sexual objects, and developing better health-care skills. Since women are redefining their gender roles faster than men, many men are then put in positions of exploring, understanding and altering their own gender roles. Positive maleness, combining tenderness and toughness and treating women with respect and as equals, is a desirable outcome from this change process.

GENDER AWARE HELPING APPROACHES

Undoubtedly, the rise of feminism and the start of a men's movement have already influenced many helpers of both sexes to undertake counselling and helping with a greater focus on healing psychological distress stemming from restrictive gender-role socialization and sexism.

Earlier in this chapter, I presented a statement of multicultural counselling competencies. This statement can be adapted for gender aware counselling competencies, which consist of three main dimensions: awareness of own assumptions, values and biases, understanding the worldview of the sex-different helpee, and developing appropriate strategies and techniques. The basic assumption in stating these competencies is that all helpers need to address their own levels of gender awareness and ability to offer gender-sensitive services.

Feminist counselling and helping is a prominent approach to addressing gender issues. Feminist helpers subscribe to many different theoretical orientations. Feminist helping is perhaps best described by the values or principles that have emerged from the joining of feminism with counselling. Box 27.1 describes five such central principles underlying feminist helping.

BOX 27.1   FIVE CENTRAL PRINCIPLES OF FEMINIST HELPING

1 **Egalitarian relationships**   Feminist helpers are extremely sensitive to issues of power and its distribution. They emphasize sharing power with helpees, and believe that hierarchical forms of power distribution are inappropriate. Self-disclosure of one's own experiences as a woman can be an important part of the counselling process.
2 **Pluralism**   Feminist theory acknowledges and values difference, including complex and multiple-level diversities. Respect for others, including their differences, is a basic tenet of feminist helping.
3 **Working against oppression**   Feminist helpers work against all forms of oppression: for instance, on the basis of sex, sexual/affectionate orientation, race, culture, religious belief, lifestyle choice, and physical disability.

4 **External emphasis** External factors, such as social/political/economic structures, are crucial to shaping the views of women, how they see themselves, and
how others see them. Women as individuals are shaped by and interact with
political, environmental, institutional and cultural factors.

5 **Valuing women's experiences** Relying on the actual experiences of women
for descriptions of 'reality'. Grounding knowledge claimed about women on the
actual women's experience. Valuing highly the experience of women rather than
ignoring or discounting it and assuming men's experience to be normative.

What are some specific interventions in dealing with women helpees?
Interventions commonly cited by feminist helpers include challenging
sex-role stereotypes, challenging patriarchal norms, assertiveness training, strategies to encourage a sense of empowerment, and self-disclosure.
Needless to say, many women helpees bring specific problems to helping
for which gender-related strategies can be, but not always are, irrelevant.

An issue in feminist counselling and helping is whether and how to con-
front helpees with issues of sexism. You may also need to help women to
anticipate and to deal with the consequences of changing their gender
roles. One danger of bringing up issues of sexism too soon is that helpees
resist the explanation and do not see its relevance. The opposite is also possible, in that they simplistically latch on to a sexist oppression analysis of
their situations, get extremely angry with their partners, and prematurely
leave them rather than attempt to work through their relationship issues.

The men's movement is the other, and sometimes missing, half of the
women's movement. There needs to be a greater development of men's
helping to complement – and definitely not to compete against – responsible
feminist helping. Since women and girls easily outnumber men and boys
as helpees, probably many helpers and helping services need to become
more user-friendly for males and skilled at working with the specific issues
facing them. For instance, more attention needs to be paid to what influences boys and men in seeking help. With some adaptation, the five
central principles of feminist helping – egalitarian relationships, pluralism,
working against oppression, external emphasis, and valuing the experience of one's own sex – are highly relevant for men's counselling and
helping too.

As with multicultural counselling competencies, as a beginning helper
you cannot be expected to learn everything at once. Gaining an initial
awareness of how gender considerations can influence basic counselling
skills, such as active listening and asking questions, is a good place to start
in becoming a genuinely gender aware and sensitive helper.

Activity 27.1   Multicultural helping

PART A: MY CULTURE AND HELPING

1 From which ancestral culture or cultures are you?
2 What distinctive values and ways of thinking, communicating and acting, stemming from your ancestral culture(s), do you possess?

PART B: MULTICULTURAL HELPING GOALS

Look at the section of the chapter on multicultural helping goals. What goals for multicultural helping do you consider particularly relevant for either your present or future helping work?

PART C: MULTICULTURAL HELPING COMPETENCIES

What competencies or skills do you think you need to develop to make you better at assisting helpees from different cultures?

Activity 27.2   Gender aware helping

PART A: MY GENDER-ROLE IDENTITY

1 How do you describe yourself on the dimensions of 'masculinity' and 'femininity'?
2 Succinctly summarize your gender-role identity.

PART B: GENDER AWARE HELPING GOALS

1 What are some special problems that girls and women bring to helping?
2 What are some special problems that boys and men bring to helping?
3 What are some goals for gender aware helping?

   • for both sexes
   • for girls and women; and
   • for boys and men.

PART C: GENDER AWARE HELPING COMPETENCIES

What competencies or skills do you think you need to develop to make you better at assisting helpees from a different gender to you?

GETTING SUPPORT AND BEING SUPERVISED

28

CHAPTER GOALS

By studying and doing the activity in this chapter you should:

- Know some ways of getting support.
- Develop some skills of presenting material in and making use of supervision.

Since many helpers who use basic counselling skills may not have access to formal supervision arrangements, I divide this chapter into two overlapping parts: getting support and being supervised.

GETTING SUPPORT

There are many reasons why you may not have access to formal supervision arrangements to build your counselling skills. You may be using counselling skills as part of other primary roles, for instance teaching, nursing or offering financial advice. In such situations, resources for staff support and development may focus on their primary tasks rather than on your counselling activities. Providing supervision to monitor and build employees' counselling skills can be expensive and time-consuming, and employers may neither have nor perceive that they have sufficient funds for this purpose. Furthermore, some institutions and agencies attach a low priority to the use of counselling skills by their employees, instead preferring them to take more direct approaches.

In work and voluntary agency settings, apart from formal supervision, there are a number of ways in which you can gain valuable support and assistance in building your counselling skills. You may be assigned to bosses or mentors with whom you review work on a regular basis or seek help from when you feel you need it. You may also be part of teams that meet on a regular basis in staff meetings and case conferences to discuss how to deal with helpees. In such instances, you may have access to skilled team leaders who can both teach you how to improve your basic counselling skills and also draw on the experience of the other group members to provide enriched learning environments.

In addition, work settings or voluntary agencies may run special workshops or short courses to assist you to develop specific skills for dealing with special clienteles. Furthermore, the settings in which you use counselling skills may have their own support systems of competent professionals with whom you can discuss individual helpees.

In instances of inadequate provision of support from institutions and agencies, you can identify more experienced colleagues to act as informal mentors. In addition, you can consider forming your own peer support group. On occasion, you may be forced to look outside your employing institution or agency to obtain suitable professional advice, for instance from trusted counselling professionals or psychiatrists. In such instances, be guided by the best interests of helpees and be very sensitive to protecting their rights to confidentiality. In addition, as discussed in Chapter 15, where you and your mentors feel out of your depth, you often have the option of referring helpees to those more suitably qualified. However, this is not always the case.

BEING SUPERVISED

You require competent supervision to develop your counselling skills well. Supervision literally means overseeing. You can discuss your use of counselling skills with experienced practitioners who can assist you to develop your effectiveness. A distinction exists between 'training supervision' and 'consultative supervision'. Training supervision is part of the ongoing training of helping students both on courses and when on probation. Consultative supervision is an egalitarian arrangement between one or more qualified helpers who meet together for the purposes of improving the practice of at least one of them. The major emphasis in the remainder of this chapter is on how to benefit from regular and systematic training supervision.

GOALS AND FORMATS FOR SUPERVISION

The overriding goal of supervision is to assist those supervised to think and communicate as effective helpers and, in so doing, to become your own *internal* supervisor. Early on, supervisors may have to do some 'hand holding' as they assist you in breaking the ice with real helpees. In addition, you can receive help from your supervisors to assist you to examine and address poor mind skills contributing to performance anxiety. Throughout supervision, supervisees should receive emotional support in a way that encourages self-reliance and honest self-appraisal rather than dependence and a need for supervisor approval.

Supervisions can take place either one-to-one, or with two or more helping trainees or helpers. Resources permitting, my preference, especially when you start seeing helpees, is for individual supervision. Advantages of individual supervision include providing you with adequate time to be supervised thoroughly and the fact that many of you are more likely to discuss sensitive issues regarding helpees and yourself than if supervised with others.

Small group supervision also has some advantages. For example, you may get exposure to a greater range of helpees and develop skills of discussing and receiving feedback on your work from peers as well as from your supervisor. Furthermore, some of you may be more self-disclosing in the context of other supervisees' honest appraisals of your performance.

A combination of participating in individual supervision and in counselling-skills training groups has much to recommend it. You can learn assessment skills and different helping strategies in training groups. Furthermore, in such groups you can share your experiences of working with helpees in ways that may be beneficial for all concerned.

To some extent the supervision process parallels the helping process, in that supervisors should develop good collaborative relationships with you to provide fertile contexts in which to monitor and improve your skills. In supervision, however, the emphasis is on improving the mind skills and the communication skills required for effective helping rather than on managing personal problems.

The supervision literature is full of references to counter-transference, the process by which helpers distort how they perceive and behave towards helpees to meet their own needs. For instance, supervisees and even experienced helpers too may, at varying levels of awareness, be encouraging dependency, sexual interest or even distance in some helpees. Effective supervision assists you to identify, explore and address such distortions, at least insofar as they affect your work. Supervisors should also identify and address their own counter-transference distortions towards those whom they supervise.

PRESENTING MATERIAL IN SUPERVISION

The following are some methods whereby you can present helping session content in supervision sessions. Some of these methods can be used in combination to add to the validity of understanding what actually transpired.

- *Verbal report* Verbal reporting on its own relies entirely on memory, which will certainly be incomplete and will almost certainly be highly selective. The greater the period of time between sessions and supervision, the more invalid memory may become. Furthermore, if you are seeing other helpees, it becomes difficult to remember exactly what happened with whom.

- *Process notes*   Process notes, if written up immediately after helping sessions and using a structured format, do not rely so heavily on memory. Such notes can act as an aid to memory during supervisions. The combination of process notes and verbal report, while still open to a high degree of invalidity, is probably more valid than relying on verbal report alone.
- *Audio recording*   Audio recording means that there is a valid record of all the verbal and vocal content of sessions. Another advantage of audio recording is that either you can choose or supervisors can request specific segments on which to focus. Audio recording can be relatively unobtrusive when only a small microphone is visible.
- *Video recording*   Video recording has the great advantage over audio recording in that there is a valid record of bodily as well as verbal and vocal session content. Viewing video recordings of sessions is my preferred way of conducting supervisions. However, some placements may not be set up for video recording, in which case audio recording is the next best choice. A possible disadvantage of video recording is that the machinery tends to be much more obtrusive than that required for audio recording.
- *Role-playing*   Where video recording is not available, role-playing can provide a way of finding out how supervisees actually communicate. You can orient your supervisor to the helpee's role and then counsel the supervisor as 'helpee' in a way that resembles part of the actual session.
- *Helpee feedback*   Helpees can provide feedback relevant to understanding what happened in helping sessions in a number of ways. Supervisors and supervisees should take note of and try to understand the reasons for single sessions and for missed appointments. Towards the end of helping sessions, you can ask helpees to provide feedback about the helping relationship and procedures. They can also fill out brief post-session questionnaires asking them for similar feedback.

MAKING USE OF SUPERVISION

Supervision sessions can be broken down into three stages: preparation, the supervision session itself, and follow-up. In the preparation stage, you can do such things as write up and reflect on your session notes and go through audio recordings or video recordings, selecting excerpts for presentation of use of good and poor counselling skills. In addition, you can read up on possible helping strategies, think about issues connected with differences between yourself and your helpees, ponder ethical issues, and in other ways reflect upon how you can make the most of your supervision time.

Early in sessions, you and your supervisor can establish a session agenda. Sometimes, you only get one supervision hour for five or eight hours of contact. If recording is used, important decisions include which recordings to present and, for those chosen, which excerpts to review. When working with recordings, a risk is that so much time is spent on the first few minutes of a session that later work in sessions either receives insufficient attention or none.

In Chapter 17, I mentioned the importance of using helpee-centred coaching skills with helpees. You may gain from similar skills being employed by your supervisors during your time together. Sometimes, supervisors may wish to stop recordings to point something out. However, on many occasions, supervisees should be the ones to choose which excerpts to present and when to stop for discussion. Supervisors can facilitate the process by asking questions such as 'What was going on there?', 'What were you trying to do?', 'What were you feeling?' and 'What skills were you using and how well were you using them?' Within the context of good collaborative relationships, supervisors develop your skills of thinking systematically about your helping work so that you become your own internal supervisor. Towards the end of supervision sessions both participants can review its main points and negotiate any specific homework assignments.

The follow-up stage of a supervision session has two main goals. One goal is that of using in your next sessions with helpees the improved skills you discussed and worked on in supervision. Another goal is that of carrying out specific homework assignments. For instance, you and your supervisor may agree that you should practise a specific helping strategy before using it. A further assignment might be reading some specific references relevant to particular helpees' problems. Supervision homework can also focus on improving your mind skills and not just those of helpees. For example, you can agree to spend time challenging and restating any demanding rule or rules that contribute to your performance anxiety.

Supervisees vary in ability to make the most out of supervision. Some may not be prepared to work hard at achieving competence. Others have personal problems of such magnitude that possibly they should not be counselling helpees at all until their own life is in better shape. It is particularly hard to supervise trainees who are defensive and possess little insight into how their poor mind and communication skills interfere with their helping. Some supervisees are difficult to supervise because, in varying degrees, they know it all already. A minority of supervisees initiate and/or engage in unethical behaviour, be it with their helpees or their supervisors.

Activity 28.1   Getting support and being supervised

1 Apart from formal supervision, in what ways can you get support in building your counselling and helping skills?
2 Critically discuss the advantages and disadvantages of each of the following ways of presenting material in supervision:

  • verbal reports
  • process notes
  • audio recording
  • video recording
  • role-playing
  • helpee feedback.

3 Are you satisfied with the current supervision you are receiving and, if not, what – if anything – can you do to improve the situation?

BECOMING MORE SKILLED

Once you acquire some basic counselling skills, you are challenged to become even more skilled. However, you will work in numerous contexts and roles, have widely disparate backgrounds and experience, and also differ in motivation to improve your skills. Consequently, any suggestions for becoming more skilled need to be taken in the context of your evaluation of your current counselling skills and also of your personal agendas, work requirements, and career aspirations.

BUILDING SKILLS

What are some of the methods you can use to maintain and develop your counselling skills? You can observe and listen to demonstrations by skilled counsellors and helpers. For instance, audio and video recordings of interviews conducted by leading counsellors and psychotherapists are available for purchase or hire in Britain, Australia and the United States. In Britain, films and video recordings may be hired from the British Association for Counselling and Psychotherapy (see Appendix 2). In addition, you may learn from written demonstrations of counselling skills. Transcripts of interviews by leading therapists are available, sometimes accompanying recordings. Another way you can learn from demonstration is to become the client of a skilled helper, though this should not be the primary motivation for seeking counselling help. When a graduate student in counselling at Stanford University, I learned a considerable amount about how to establish collaborative relationships from my 50 or so hours of individual therapy with a highly skilled helpee-centred counsellor.

While a whole interview approach to observing, listening to and reading transcripts is valuable, this is not the only way to approach the material. One option is to focus on smaller segments of interviews, say five minutes, and to look out for how specific counselling skills are used. In addition to verbal communication, focus on voice messages and, if observing a recording, on body messages as well.

Another option is to turn the audio or video recorder off after each helpee statement, form your own response, and then see how the helper actually responded. When working with transcripts of a session by someone like Carl Rogers, you can go down the page covering up Rogers' responses, form your own, and then check Rogers' responses. Your responses will not necessarily be inferior to those of the more famous helpers.

Co-counselling is a form of peer helping whereby in a given time period, say an hour, each person takes turns at being both helper and helpee. You can practise counselling skills with a colleague on a co-counselling basis, using audio and video feedback where appropriate. In addition, you may be able either to form or become part of a peer self-help group in which members work with, comment on, and support each other as you develop your counselling skills.

Whether in informal helping contacts or in more formal helping sessions, many of you already use counselling skills either as part of your jobs or in voluntary capacities. In some settings, you may be able to monitor yourself by recording and playing back sessions, possibly in the presence of supervisors or peers. In addition, be sensitive to feedback from helpees. Some of this feedback will entail how helpees respond with their verbal, vocal and body messages to your use of counselling skills. In addition, where appropriate, you can ask helpees for feedback on how they experienced individual sessions and about their overall helping contact with you. You can also develop your own questionnaires, however brief, to generate feedback.

TRAINING PATHS

Where do you go next if you want to gain more training in counselling skills? Many of you may be in professions, for example social work or nursing, where there may be opportunities for further training either within your existing undergraduate or postgraduate courses or, if already graduated, on in-service training courses and workshops run by your professional association or by members of it. Others of you may work in voluntary organizations that offer their own intermediate or advanced counselling-skills training courses geared to the populations that they serve.

Those of you wishing to become counsellors or counselling psychologists should look out for accredited and/or well-regarded courses. In Britain, the British Association for Counselling and Psychotherapy annually publishes *The Training in Counselling and Psychotherapy Directory*. In both Australia and Britain, the main route to becoming a counselling psychologist now is through undergraduate work in psychology, followed by a Master's in counselling psychology. Those so inclined can contact the relevant counselling psychotherapy and psychology professional association for details of accredited courses (see Appendix 2).

Graduation from a counselling, psychotherapy or counselling psychology course does not in itself mean accreditation. To obtain accreditation, graduates will be required to accumulate a set number of hours of supervised helping practice. Afterwards, to maintain accreditation, you may be required to have ongoing supervision or regularly accumulate continuing professional development points by attending conferences, workshops and training courses.

A distinction exists between accreditation by a professional association and mandatory registration or licensing by either a national registration board or, as in Australia, by a state registration board. In some states in Australia people cannot call themselves counselling psychologists unless certified as such by the relevant state registration board. In both Britain and Australia, the trend is towards tightening up the licensing of counsellors, psychotherapists and counselling psychologists. The development of the United Kingdom Register of Counsellors is an important milestone on the British landscape.

Attending conferences, short courses and workshops can provide an informal training path whereby you can improve your knowledge and skills. In Britain details of short courses, workshops and conferences can be found in the British Association for Counselling and Psychotherapy's monthly journal *Therapy Today* and in the British Psychological Society's monthly journal *The Psychologist*. Similar information is available in journals published by Australian psychology and counselling professional associations (see Appendix 2). Furthermore, in both countries information about short courses, workshops and conferences can be found in the newsletters and journals of other counselling-related professional associations, for instance those for human resource management, and of voluntary agencies, such as *Relate News* in Britain.

If you are interested in developing your counselling skills in a particular approach to helping, enquire whether there is a training centre in your locality. Most major helping approaches have international networks for training and practice. For example, agencies for specialized training in person-centred therapy exist in Britain and for rational emotive behaviour therapy in both Britain and Australia.

BOOKS AND JOURNALS

BOOKS

There is a large theoretical literature that underpins the use of counselling skills. This can be divided into primary sources, books and articles written by the leading theorists themselves, and secondary sources, book and articles written about the different theoretical approaches by people other than their originators. Ultimately, there is no substitute for reading primary sources. However, it can be a daunting task for the beginning helper to know where to start and how to cover the ground. In order to help you to access the counselling and helping literature, I have provided an Annotated Bibliography as Appendix 1 of this book.

JOURNALS

Journals provide an excellent means of keeping abreast of the counselling skills literature. Some of you are in fields such as nursing, social work and human resource management, whose professional journals may contain some articles about the use of counselling skills.

Box 29.1 provides a list of some of the main counselling and counselling psychology journals. Two of the journals – *Counselling & Psychotherapy Research* and the *Journal of Counseling Psychology* – focus mainly on research.

BOX 29.1   SOME LEADING COUNSELLING AND COUNSELLING PSYCHOLOGY JOURNALS

COUNSELLING

Australian Journal of Guidance and Counselling

British Journal of Guidance and Counselling

Therapy Today (British Association for Counselling and Psychotherapy)

Counselling and Psychotherapy Research (British Association for Counselling and Psychotherapy)

Journal of Counseling and Development (American Association for Counselling)

New Zealand Counselling and Guidance Association Journal

International Journal for the Advancement of Counselling

(Continued)

(Continued)

COUNSELLING PSYCHOLOGY

The Australian Counselling Psychologist (Australian Psychological Society)

Counselling Psychology Review (British Psychological Society)

Journal of Counseling Psychology (American Psychological Association)

The Counseling Psychologist (American Psychological Association)

PERSONAL COUNSELLING AND SELF-HELP

PERSONAL COUNSELLING

Some of you will have been clients before embarking on basic counselling-skills training and may still be continuing in counselling. Reasons to consider undergoing counselling include personal growth, gaining understanding of the helpee's position, and extending your experience of types of therapy.

Personal counselling can be very beneficial in working through blocks to being a happier, more fulfilled and humane person. In addition, you may address material in personal counselling related to your placements and supervision, for instance, fears about dealing with certain kinds of helpees and tendencies towards over-involvement or under-involvement. Either in addition to or instead of individual counselling, those of you wishing to deal with past deprivations and current problems can also consider undertaking couples, family or group modes of counselling. Furthermore, participating in lifeskills training groups, for instance focused on assertiveness skills or managing stress skills, can help some to become stronger and more skilled human beings.

An issue in counsellor and helper training is whether undergoing personal counselling should be mandatory. Above I have presented some ways in which personal counselling might be beneficial. However, there is another side to the issue. Reservations about making personal counselling a criterion for the accreditation of counsellors and helpers include relevance, coercion, cost, defining the minimum length, and insufficient research evidence. Regarding relevance, counselling approaches differ in the importance they attach to trainees undergoing personal counselling. Regarding coercion, counselling is not necessarily going to be effective when in response to a bureaucratic demand. Regarding cost, adding the costs of personal counselling to the expense of helper training leads to elitism and discriminates against poorer trainees. Regarding the required length of counselling necessary, approaches differ on how long this should be, if at all. Finally, regarding the research evidence for the effectiveness of personal counselling in enhancing helping practice, the case has still to be decisively proven.

SELF-HELP

Counselling skills training can provide you with some useful tools for improving your own functioning. When reflecting upon the experiences of your daily life, you can treat yourself as a helpee. You are still the same person in your everyday roles, for instance as partners or parents, as in your helping role. Sometimes, self-help is best done systematically: for example, clear sufficient temporal, physical and psychological space within which to create a collaborative relationship with yourself. Next clarify and expand your understanding of what is going on in problem situations. During this process you can identify unhelpful thoughts and communication/actions and translate these into specific mind skills and communication/action skills to improve. Then, applying some of the helping strategies described in this book to yourself, work to improve your effectiveness.

As time goes by, you are likely to get wise to characteristic poor mind skills and communication/action skills that you employ. For example, you may develop skills at dissipating self-defeating anger through identifying, challenging and, if necessary, restating a demanding rule that was creating much of your anger. You can also become adept at retrieving mistakes you make in your private life by acknowledging them and then using appropriate mind and communication skills to get back on track.

In addition to working on your own, you can be part of peer self-help groups and support networks. For example, members of women's groups, men's groups, gay and lesbian groups, and groups composed of members of specific ethnic minorities can help each other to develop more of one's humanity and to deal with personal, institutional and political oppression.

Activity 29.1   Becoming more skilled

Below are some ways that you may choose to help you to become more skilled. Which ones are suitable for you?

1: BUILDING SKILLS

The following are some methods you may choose to use:

* observing and listening to video and audio recordings
* reading transcripts of interviews

(Continued)

(Continued)

- co-counselling
- peer self-help groups
- feedback from supervisors, peers and helpees
- questionnaires.

2: TRAINING PATHS

What are the opportunities for further training available to you?

3: BOOKS AND JOURNALS

- What books might you read to help you to become more skilled? Some books are listed in Appendix 1.
- What journals might you look at to help you to become more skilled? See Box 29.1 for some ideas.

4: PERSONAL COUNSELLING AND SELF-HELP

- Do you think you might enter personal counselling to contribute to helping yourself become more skilled?
- What methods of self-help might contribute to your becoming more skilled?

APPENDIX 1
ANNOTATED BIBLIOGRAPHY

Alberti, R. and Emmons, M. (2008) *Your Perfect Right: Assertiveness and Equality in Your Life and Relationships,* 9th edn. Atascadero, CA: Impact Publishers.
This popular book is divided into three parts: You and your perfect right, Discovering assertiveness, and Becoming assertive.

Bond, T. (2015) *Standards and Ethics for Counselling in Action*, 4th edn. London: Sage.
This book consists of four parts – The background, Responsibility to the client, The counsellor and others, and The whole picture. Highly recommended as an introduction to ethical issues and dilemmas in helping.

Chaplin, J. (1999) *Feminist Counselling in Action*, 2nd edn. London: Sage.
This book presents a multi-stage rhythm model of feminist therapy. Chaplin illustrates each stage of the process with three case studies.

D'Ardenne, P. and Mahtani, A. (1999) *Transcultural Counselling in Action,* 2nd edn. London: Sage.
This book is written by two clinical psychologists, one with a white English and the other with an Indian background, working in London's East End. The book introduces the concept of transcultural counselling and then reviews practical issues concerned with helpees, counsellors, starting the counselling process, sharing a common language, the therapeutic relationship, change and growth, and ending counselling. The book is illustrated by four case studies of helpees with Bangladeshi, English, French and Nigerian cultural backgrounds.

Egan, G. (2013) *The Skilled Helper: A Problem-Management and Opportunity-Development Approach to Helping*, 10th edn. Belmont, CA: Thomson Brooks/Cole.
Egan's text emphasizes the collaborative nature of the therapist–helpee relationship. Its three parts are: Laying the groundwork, The therapeutic dialogue: communication and relationship-building skills, and The skilled helper problem management and opportunity-development approach to helping.

Feltham, C. and Horton, R. (eds.) (2012) *The Sage Handbook of Counselling and Psychotherapy*, 3rd edn. London: Sage.
The seven parts of this book are: Counselling and psychotherapy in context, Socio-cultural perspectives, Therapeutic skills and clinical practice, Professional issues, Theory and approaches, Client presenting problems, and Specialisms and modalities.

Mearns, D., Thorne, B. with McLeod, J. (2013) *Person-Centred Counselling in Action*, 4th edn. London: Sage.
Engagingly written this bestselling text introduces person-centred theory and practice. Mearns and Thorne write the book's first nine chapters, whose titles are: Basic theory of the person-centred approach, Recent developments in person-centred theory, The counsellor's use of the self, Empathy, Unconditional positive regard, Congruence, 'Beginnings', 'Middles', and 'Endings'. The tenth and final chapter, written by McLeod, is entitled Research on person-centred counselling.

Nelson-Jones, R. (2014) *Practical Counselling and Helping Skills: Text and Activities for the Lifeskills Counselling Model*, 6th edn. London: Sage.
The book consists of five parts. Part one introduces the reader to what counselling and helping is, what communication skills are, feelings and mind skills, and the lifeskills counselling model. Parts two, three and four describe the skills involved in the relating stage, the understanding stage and the changing stage of the model, respectively. Numerous interventions are described for changing helpees' communications/actions, thinking, and feelings and physical reactions. Part five focuses on practice and training issues, such as multicultural, gender-aware and technology-mediated counselling and helping, ethical issues, supervision and personal counselling, and professional development.

Nelson-Jones, R. (2015) *Nelson-Jones' Theory and Practice of Counselling and Therapy*, 6th edn. London: Sage.
This comprehensive textbook consists of 18 chapters: Creating counselling and therapy approaches, Freud's psychoanalysis, Jung's analytical therapy, Person-centred therapy, Gestalt therapy, Transactional analysis, Existential therapy, Behaviour therapy, Rational emotive behaviour therapy, Cognitive therapy, Multimodal therapy, Solution-focused therapy, Narrative therapy, Positive therapy, Mindfulness in therapy, Multicultural therapy, Gender therapy, and Evaluation, eclecticism and integration.

Padesky, C.A. and Greenberger, D. (1995) *Clinician's Guide to Mind Over Mood*; and Greenberger, D. and Padesky, C.A. (1995) *Mind Over Mood: Change How You Feel by Changing the Way You Think*. New York: Guilford Press.

These companion volumes are designed as step-by-step guides to the techniques and strategies of cognitive therapy. The manual is designed as a self-help workbook and the clinician's guide provides therapists with instructions on how to incorporate the workbook into individual and group psychotherapy.

Rogers, C.R. (1961) *On Becoming a Person: A Therapist's View of Psychotherapy*. Boston, MA: Houghton Mifflin.
Regarded by Rogers as one of his most significant publications and certainly his most popular one. The book comprises seven parts: Speaking personally, How can I be of help?, The process of becoming a person, A philosophy of persons, The place of research in psychotherapy, What are the implications for living?, and The behavioural sciences and the person.

Rogers, C.R. (1980) *A Way of Being*. Boston, MA: Houghton Mifflin.
A collection of 15 papers written between 1960 and 1980, this book is divided into four parts: Personal experiences and perspectives, Aspects of a person-centred approach, The process of education – and its future and Looking ahead – a person-centred scenario. This book is written in the same reader-friendly style as *On Becoming a Person*.

Sue, D.W., Carter, R.T., Casas, J.M., Fouad, N.A., Ivey, A.E., Jensen, M., LaFromboise, T., Manese, J.E., Ponterotto, J.G. and Vazquez-Nutall, E. (1998) *Multicultural Counseling Competencies: Individual and Organizational Development*. London: Sage.
This American book introduces the concepts of multiculturalism and ethnocentric mono-culturalism and then presents the multicultural counselling competencies. Chapters follow on understanding the Euro-American worldview and on understanding racial/ethnic minority worldviews. Much of the remainder of the book focuses on multicultural organizational development, with the final chapter looking at issues of personal, professional and organizational multicultural competence.

Wedding, D. and Corsini, R.J. (2014) *Current Psychotherapies*, 10th edn. Belmont, CA: Thomson Brooks/Cole.
This well-established textbook consists of 16 chapters: Introduction to 21st century psychotherapies, Psychoanalytic psychotherapies, Adlerian psychotherapy, Client-centred therapy, Rational emotive behaviour therapy, Behaviour therapy, Cognitive therapy, Existential psychotherapy, Gestalt therapy, Interpersonal psychotherapy, Family therapy, Contemplative psychotherapies, Positive psychotherapy, Integrative psychotherapies, Multicultural theories of psychotherapy, and Contemporary challenges and controversies.

Westbrook, D., Kennerley, H. and Kirk, J. (2011) *An Introduction to Cognitive Behaviour Therapy: Skills and Applications*, 2nd edn. London: Sage.
The 19 chapters include: Distinctive characteristics of CBT, The therapeutic relationship, Assessment and formulation, Cognitive techniques, Behavioural experiments, and The course of therapy.

Wills, F. (2014) *Skills in Cognitive Behaviour Therapy*, 2nd edn. London: Sage.
This book's contents are: Practising CBT skills within their knowledge base, Assessing, formulating and starting CBT, Developing the relationship in CBT, Intervening in cognitions, Intervening in behaviours, Intervening in emotions, Intervening in lifelong patterns, and Maintaining and developing CBT skills.

Woolfe, R., Strawbridge, S., Douglas, B. and Dryden, W. (2010) *Handbook of Counselling Psychology,* 3rd edn. London: Sage.
This large book consists of seven parts: What is counselling psychology?, Tradition, challenge and change, Difference and discrimination, Developmental themes, Opportunities and tensions in different context, Professional and ethical issues, and Future opportunities and challenges.

BRITAIN

British Association for Counselling and Psychotherapy
BACP House
15 St John's Business Park
Lutterworth
Leicestershire LE17 4HB
 Tel: 01455-883300
 Fax: 01455-550243
 E-mail: bacp@bacp.co.uk
 Website: www.bacp.co.uk

British Psychological Society
St Andrews House
48 Princess Road East
Leicester LE1 7DR
 Tel: 0116-254-9568
 Fax: 0116-227-1314
 E-mail: mail@bps.org.uk
 Website: www.bps.org.uk

United Kingdom Council for Psychotherapy
2nd Floor, Edward House
2 Wakley Street
London EC1V 7LT
 Tel: 020-7014-9955
 Fax: 020-7014-9977
 E-mail: info@ukcp.org.uk
 Website: www.psychotherapy.org.uk

AUSTRALIA

Australian Psychological Society
PO Box 38
Flinders Lane Post Office
Melbourne
Victoria 8009
  Tel: 03-8662-3300
  Fax: 03-9663-6177
  E-mail: contactus@psychology.org.au
  Website: www.psychology.org.au

Psychotherapy and Counselling Federation of Australia
290 Park Street
Fitzroy North, Melbourne
Victoria 3068
  Tel: 03-9486-3077
  Fax: 03-9486-3933
  E-mail: admin@pacfa.org.au
  Website: www.pacfa.org.au

USA

American Counseling Association
5999 Stevenson Avenue
Alexandria
VA 22304
  Tel: 800-347-6647
  Fax: 800-473-2329
  Website: www.counseling.org

American Psychological Association
750 First Street NE
Washington
DC 20002-4242
  Tel: 800-374-2721 or 202-336-5500
  Website: www.apa.org

INDEX

CPSIA information can be obtained
at www.ICGtesting.com
Printed in the USA
JSHW042132100123
35818JS00007B/149